Discourses of Borders and the Nation in the USA

This book introduces an innovative critical analysis of borders in contemporary political discourse, using examples from the Trump presidency and early stages of the Biden presidency to explore how borders are used as mechanisms of power to invoke different notions of national identity.

This volume considers borders as discursive constructs, reflecting on their importance in the construction and expression of national identity across different forms of modern political discourse. Employing a framework informed by Ruth Wodak's Discourse-Historical Approach, Demata examines how analysing discourse from the Trump and Biden presidencies can reveal unique insights into how politicians use borders to recontextualise historical discourses of national identity and employ discursive strategies of inclusion and exclusion in promoting the idea of the nation. In adopting an approach which situates these discourses within their historical and socio-cultural contexts, the volume helps to further bridge the gap between different disciplines and offers a multi-faceted understanding of notions of borders and national identity in contemporary political language.

This book will be of interest to students and scholars in the fields of discourse analysis, language and power, language and politics, political science, and border studies.

Massimiliano Demata is Associate Professor of English at the University of Turin. He took his DPhil in English in Oxford (1999), was a Fulbright scholar in Yale (1999) and Indiana University (2014), and has lectured as Visiting Professor at Saarland University (2020), Sciences Po Lyon (2021) and OTH Regensburg (2022). He is the co-editor of the *Journal of Language and Discrimination* and has published extensively on populist discourse, Trump's rhetoric, metaphors of the nation and social media discourse.

Discourses of Borders and the Nation in the USA
A Discourse-Historical Analysis

Massimiliano Demata

Routledge
Taylor & Francis Group

NEW YORK AND LONDON

First published 2023
by Routledge
605 Third Avenue, New York, NY 10158

and by Routledge
4 Park Square, Milton Park, Abingdon, Oxon, OX14 4RN

Routledge is an imprint of the Taylor & Francis Group, an informa business

© 2023 Massimiliano Demata

The right of Massimiliano Demata to be identified as author of this work
has been asserted in accordance with sections 77 and 78 of the Copyright,
Designs and Patents Act 1988.

Library of Congress Cataloging-in-Publication Data
A catalog record for this title has been requested

ISBN: 9781032263687 (hbk)
ISBN: 9781032263694 (pbk)
ISBN: 9781003287971 (ebk)

DOI: 10.4324/9781003287971

Typeset in Baskerville
by Newgen Publishing UK

Contents

Acknowledgements

This book could not have been written without the assistance, advice, encouragement or teaching of many people, some of them both colleagues and friends, who have helped me at various stages and degrees of my long, slow and often frustrating writing path. I would like to thank Michelangelo Conoscenti, who is more than just a friend and a colleague and who has believed in me from day one of our friendship; Astrid Fellner and Eva Nossem at Saarland University, who welcomed me as a Visiting Professor at Saarland University in 2020 and gave me the opportunity to start working on my book; Elisabeth Vallet, with whom I have worked several times in the last three years and who made the term "interdisciplinarity" a concrete reality; Thierry Fortin, who gave me the opportunity to teach a postgraduate course on "Discourses of Borders: nations, walls, security" at Sciences Po Lyon in September–October 2021; and my students at the University of Turin and Sciences Po Lyon. I also owe a debt of gratitude to Giuseppe Balirano, Elena Di Giovanni and Marianna Zummo, without whose encouragement this book would not have been finished. I would also like to thank Harry Dixon and Elysse Preposi at Routledge: their help and patience have been crucial in having my initial book proposal accepted and in enabling me to complete this book. Finally, I would like to thank the three people who have been central to my academic and personal life. I am enormously indebted to Ruth Wodak: her writings opened, to quote William Blake, the doors of perception to the complexities and intricacies of discourse, and (unbeknown to her!) she has always been the model and lodestar for my research; last, but first really, my wife Jole and my daughter Grace have patiently coped with my frequent distractions from family life, have constantly supported me, and have unfailingly showed me that there is always love, joy and happiness in life beyond academia.

Introduction

In the last, revised chapter of the second edition of his epochal *Nations and Nationalism since 1780*, Eric Hobsbawm reflected on the resurgence of nationalism on the basis of the new nations born out of the collapse of the Soviet Union as well as the new nationalist movements—such as Jean-Marie Le Pen's National Front in France—and their ethnocentric tendencies. Many such nationalist movements were openly based on xenophobia as well as, often, racism. Hobsbawm argued:

> What is the nature of this cry of distress or fury? Time and again such movements of ethnic identity seem to be reactions of weakness and fear, attempts to erect barricades to keep at bay the forces of the modern world (…) What fuels such defensive reactions, whether against real or imaginary threats, is a combination of international population movements with the ultra-rapid, fundamental and unprecedented socio-economic transformations so characteristic of the third quarter of our century.
>
> (1992: 170–171)

One cannot fail to spot an eerie resemblance between Hobsbawm's reflections on the racism-infused nationalism of the late twentieth century and what is happening in many nations in the first segment of the twenty-first century. While there have obviously been many changes in the world's social and political scenario, the new populist leaders—Donald J. Trump, Nigel Farage, Boris Johnson, Marine Le Pen, Matteo Salvini, Viktor Orbán and many others—are appealing to "real or imaginary threats," their programme being based on the need to protect the nation from "the forces of the modern world" by "erect[ing] barricades." One wonders whether Hobsbawm was aware that the war image implied in his use of "barricade" could also be taken literally: the world of nations and the ideology of nationalism are founded on a fixed distinction between "our" nation and

DOI: 10.4324/9781003287971-1

all other nations, and this distinction has increasingly been made visible, geopolitically as well as physically, by strong, militarised borders, often in the shape of walls.

The force of attraction exercised on the electorate by populist movements, parties and leaders in many countries worldwide relies, in many respects, on the same "cry of distress and fury" that Hobsbawm identified in the early 1990s, and has prompted very similar (or even stronger) reactions of closure of, and exclusion from, the nation and its borders. With the current wave of populism and nationalism, borders have once again become the focus of politics and all the discourses related to it. This is particularly relevant when we look at contemporary populist narratives of the nation: these narratives focus on fear, risk and danger evolving around certain threats (imaginary, exaggerated or real) to the integrity of the nation and its inhabitants. A nation is represented as under threat if and when its borders are crossed by threatening "strangers" of some sort or another, in a continuation (or at least a new cycle) of the nativist tendencies which Hobsbawm perceived three decades ago.

This book addresses the role played by borders as a key discourse topic of the narratives of the nation which have emerged in the USA during and after the presidency of Donald J. Trump. More specifically, I have analysed borders in the discourse of the last two US presidents, Trump and Joe Biden, and of two key progressive politicians, Bernie Sanders and Hillary Clinton. This choice derives from the awareness that, in the public sphere (in the Habermasian sense of the term) in the USA and elsewhere, borders play a key role in the discourses of the nation. Analysing the discourse structures and strategies used to represent them can shed light on how a nation is conceptualised, and even visualised, by its citizens. This is particularly true in what should be considered as the most influential (and, in terms of the social order of a nation, hegemonic) discourse domain, that is politics. If notions such as the "Trump Wall," "hard border," "smart borders," "porous borders" and "border security" have become so frequent both in specialised discourses (e.g. in Geopolitics and in Border Studies) and at the popular level through the media and among the electorate, this is also due to the way they are structured and recontextualised in discourse. As what US politicians say or write is inevitably prioritised in the order of discourse, they are bound to be influential in society: their statements about borders inevitably condition citizens' perceptions of borders as well as of their own nation.

This book is based on the assumption that the function of borders is not merely institutional, but is part of a process in which the concept of the nation is continually naturalised and legitimised *through discourse*. Accordingly, this book attempts to fulfil the need for an interdisciplinary approach capable of accounting for the complex recontextualisations that take place in the discourses of the nation when addressing borders. To this purpose, I have employed the Discourse-Historical Approach (DHA), a branch of Critical Discourse Analysis developed by Ruth Wodak and her research network. The DHA explains discourse and its structures in the wider historical and social and cultural context of text production. The DHA has proved very effective in identifying and analysing the strategies behind discourses of racism and discrimination and the links between ideologies, discourses and texts. I believe this is necessary to develop an approach to discourse as a foundational component of society, as well as to overcome the inevitable limitations that single disciplines might have in dealing with borders. Indeed, if the difference between the ontology of borders (what borders are) and the epistemology of borders (the study of what we know about borders and how we know them) has collapsed (van Houtum 2005), then borders must be studied in terms of how they are conceptualised within discourse communities, rather than only in their institutional function as lines drawn between nations and legitimised through international relations. While they may seem fixed and eternal, borders, like nations or any other social institution, are not a "given" that exists unchallenged and in eternity. Their role is constantly negotiated within society, as they often become major talking points for groups who compete for social, cultural and political hegemony in a nation. Clearly, then, an understanding of how borders are *represented and understood* in society is as important as what borders actually *are*. It is through discourse that certain notions about borders are construed. It is through discourse that the meaning of borders in the social and cultural understanding of the nation is negotiated. And it is through discourses about borders that a sense of uniqueness in "our" collective national identity is constructed in opposition to "other" identities.

The first part of the book gives an outline of the modern developments of the concept of borders in nationalist milieux and in border studies. This two-pronged route to addressing borders is essential in order to understand how borders function in society, and specifically in the representations of the nation in political discourse. As an object of research, borders must be regarded not as a *fait accompli*, that is as a "given" separated from its context of use, but as a dynamic social factor in the construction of the nation whose meaning is negotiated, conceptualised and known through discourse. The core of this book consists of an analysis of the discursive strategies employed by Trump to represent borders. Borders, and particularly the very controversial Trump Wall, were at the heart of Trump's first (and, so far, only) mandate. They have been used as a key discourse topic in Trump's idea of the nation, one based mainly on security, nativism and exclusion. My argument here is that, especially through the Trump Wall, borders become central to Trump's recontextualisation of certain discourses at the core of his policies: in pairing immigration with borders, Trump constructs a logic of physical, and even visual, exclusion of those outsiders whom he represents as a threat to the nation, framing security as the key priority for US citizens. To do so, he also develops an aesthetic of borders, through his own signature wall (the "Trump Wall") and his continuous reliance on the discourse of real estate, which turns the border wall into a luxury item or an object of consumption constructed (literally and socially) to exclude those who do not deserve to enter the USA. As Chapter 3 shows, the border policies proposed by the Democrats did oppose Trump's policies, but only to a certain extent: an analysis of the dataset of texts by Hillary Clinton, Bernie Sanders and Joe Biden shows that the recontextualisation of certain discourses constructed as an alternative to the Trump Wall (i.e. open borders or the "smart border") could not avoid the strong emphasis on security (and therefore, potentially, exclusion) which is central in Trump's notion of borders.

In analysing borders in the discourse of mainstream US politics, I have adopted a qualitative rather than a quantitative approach: on the basis of their resonance and impact, I have selected what I have judged to be the most important and influential texts addressing borders by Trump, Sanders, Clinton and Biden in their official Facebook and Twitter pages, speeches, interviews, and the White House and campaign websites. Except where noted, all of Trump's tweets, Facebook posts, interviews and speeches have been taken from the Factbase website (https://factba.se/trump/).

The section on "The border wall: security and the nation" in Chapter 2 is an expansion and reworking of my article " 'A great and beautiful wall'. Donald Trump's populist discourse on immigration," *Journal of Language Aggression and Conflict* 5(2): 277–297.

1 Borders, nations and security in the age of populism

This chapter addresses the methodological approach employed in this book as a whole as well as the socio-cultural context in which recent discourses of borders in the USA have been constructed. The chosen methodology is the Discourse-Historical Approach (DHA) which, because of its interdisciplinary versatility, is ideal for analysing the role of borders in discourses of the nation: as a key topic in hegemonic discourses of the nation, borders often function as protection against unwanted "outsiders," who are represented as threatening the nation. The DHA can explain how certain structures of power, discourses and ideologies are recontextualised when talking about borders. Approaching the study of borders through the DHA can thus lead to a more thorough understanding of how social and cultural differences between (and inside) national groups are constructed in a nation's public sphere. The discussion of the methodology is followed by an analysis of the political and historical context of the notion of borders as a necessary institutional and cultural element of the nation and in its discourses. Specifically, the chapter analyses the construction of borders in discourse as the physical and ideological line of demarcation between "us" and "them": borders are used to formulate certain parameters of inclusion and exclusion in discourse. In this sense, borders have a crucial function in discourse, as their use contributes to the processes of both ordering and othering (van Houtum and van Naerssen 2001), two strategies which are central in populist and nationalist discourses. The last section of the chapter discusses the way the notion of borders seems to be dominated by the social, political and economic tension between a borderless and a bordered world. Borderlessness is one of the main features of the globalised world which seemed to be a prevailing model for international relations in the period between the fall of the Berlin Wall in 1989 and the 9/11 terrorist attacks on the Twin Towers and the Pentagon in 2001. The idea of the (newly) bordered world has gradually risen to prominence after 9/11 and witnessed a political showdown of sorts in 2016: in that year, the victory of Leave in the Brexit referendum and

DOI: 10.4324/9781003287971-2

Donald Trump's win in the US presidential elections were the catalysts of a new tendency in international relations and movements which ran counter to the globalised and neoliberal notions of free trade and movement between nations which for some had cast doubt on the very existence of borders. Hence the current penchant for "strong" borders, a concept linked to the populist obsession with crisis and national security which is most glaringly apparent in Trump's proposed border wall.

Theoretical framework and methodology: the Discourse-Historical Approach

This book's analysis of the discourses of borders is based mainly on the DHA. The DHA is a key branch of Critical Discourse Analysis (CDA), an interdisciplinary approach which has been used to critically describe, assess and explain how language establishes, legitimises and maintains social inequality (Reisigl and Wodak 2016). Among CDA's many methodologies, the DHA, as developed by Ruth Wodak and her colleagues (Reisigl and Wodak 2001, 2016; Wodak 2001, 2015; Wodak et al., 2009), proposes an interdisciplinary focus which frames discourse and its production in their socio-historical context. The DHA is thus based on *critical* discourse analysis and consists of a set of tools for analysing language and its links to those social and discourse structures which bear the imprint of social and political inequalities. Crucially, DHA goes beyond the mere analysis of language: its emphasis on the intertextual and interdiscursive relationships between texts, discourses and genres consists in the employment, in the analysis of data, of what Wodak calls triangulation between different research methods and principles. Thus, the discourse reconstruction derived from the intertextual and interdiscursive analysis (i.e. the identification of those discourses to which certain words or phrases belong) proposed by DHA enables dialogue with other disciplines and a more comprehensive view of the texts and discourses under analysis. Through its interdisciplinary approach, the DHA has often been used to analyse the key discursive elements of contemporary forms of discriminatory—e.g. racist, nationalist, populist and anti-immigration—discourses, unmasking and shedding light on their origins, incongruences and contradictions, and situating them in specific historical contexts. This, for example, is the case of Wodak's analysis of the racist and antisemitic discourses of European populist right-wing parties and movements (Reisigl and Wodak 2001; Wodak 2015).

Wodak considers discourse as a set of textual (linguistic) practices that are context-dependent. For this reason, the analysis of discourse must consider all these elements constituting context itself because there are always dialogic relations between the micro-level of language and the social and ideological macro-structures (KhosraviNik 2010). Wodak states that the DHA is three-dimensional: first, "the specific *content or topic(s)* of a specific discourse" are identified, after which "*discursive strategies*" are investigated, followed by an examination of "*linguistic means* (as types) and context-dependent *linguistic realizations* (as tokens)" (Reisigl and Wodak 2016: 32, emphasis in the original). Each text belonging to a given discourse includes one or more discourse topics, which are shared with other texts that are part of the same discourse and, often, intersect with different discourses. In the DHA, three dimensions of analysis account for the contextual col-location and understanding of texts: intertextuality, interdiscursivity and field of action (Wodak 2001: 66–67; Reisigl and Wodak 2016: 27–28). Intertextuality and interdiscursivity are the manifestation of a more general process of recontextualisation, whereby processes of historical change take place. Recontextualisation indicates movements of elements of language and discourse between different locations, between "sites of production and reception of discourse" (Van Dijk 1991) and attests to the fact that discourses can be applied, transferred and located in different social articulations, different contexts and different historical moments. Recontextualisation also has important ideological implications in the way discourses present and evaluate social reality:

> Hence, recontextualisation is not only a process of discourses' spatio-temporal diffusion, but essentially also a process of creating horizontal discourse orderings. Therein, some discourses not only recontextualise parts of the other, but also become tools in the process of creating and sustaining the hegemony of certain discursive frames.
>
> (Krzyżanowski 2016: 314)

Intertextuality is a more text-specific process: while interdiscursivity incorporates pre-existing discourses, genres or styles into the new text, intertextuality incorporates older texts into a new text (Wodak 2010; Wodak and Fairclough 2010). Intertextual and interdiscursive analysis of the relationships among different texts, genres and discourses provides an understanding of the circulation and influence between different texts and discourses in a given text. Fields of action are segments of social reality with specific functions within discourse and embed specific discursive practices. A single field of action is defined through sets of distinct genres or subgenres. There are several fields of political action, including lawmaking procedure, formation of public attitudes, inter-party formation of attitudes, opinions and will, and political advertising (Reisigl 2008: 98–99). Each field has its own genres and subgenres (e.g. typical subgenres of political adver-tising include election programmes, election slogans, election speech and election brochures; Wodak 2001: 68; Reisigl and Wodak 2016: 29). Texts belonging to one or more genres may address different topics and, in turn, a discourse addressing a given topic can start in a specific field of action and then spread to a different one.

A key dimension of the DHA consists in identifying discursive strategies, a set of practices used in order to achieve certain aims. According to Reisigl and Wodak (2001: 44), discursive strategies are "systematic ways of using language" and need to be explored as part of the analysis of texts. In their analysis of racist discourse, Reisigl and Wodak identify five discursive strategies: (1) nomination, or how persons are referred to linguistically, that is the kind of language, for example appellations, used in discourse to identify social actors; (2) predication, or the qualities and characteristics attributed to the social actors, for example through verbs denoting their actions; (3) argumentation, or the argumentative schemes used to discriminate against the excluded persons; (4) perspectivation, or the viewpoint from which such attributions and nominations are expressed; and (5) intensification or mitigation, or how the illocutionary force of the judgements about the actors is modified (Reisigl and Wodak 2001, 2016; Wodak 2015). Analysing these five strategies is crucial in identifying the ideological motives behind discourse. For the purposes of this book, nomination and predication, that is the lexical and grammatical devices used to define the identity and the actions of the social actors, can indicate specific social realities and evaluative attributions of positive or negative traits. Similarly, *topoi*, which are central to Wodak's argumentation theory, are strategies of argumentation that are used to persuade people of the validity of some claim and are displayed in language through conditional or causal paraphrases. Wodak showed that analysing *topoi* is essential in assessing how the discriminatory practices of racism are presented as rational and convincing. When discourses are produced from a hegemonic position, such evaluations may become the norm in that they are the main conduit through which such social realities are spread and known in society. For instance, when some social actors are under the attack by a hegemonic group, the negative other-description and activities attributed to them are the key ideological structures of discourse which are instrumental to their discursive representation (and marginalisation): they are given lexical and grammatical attributes defining them as outside the official narratives and the hegemonic moral and social norms. Conversely, the same strategies can be used to portray other social actors in a positive light. In the case of racist discourse, for example, the typical populist strategy is that of portraying the "people" as a uniform community constructed discursively as a majority of the nation that is victimised or threatened by some outside group, for instance migrants or the elites.

Following Wodak's formulation of the relationship between discourses, texts and context and the analysis of the field of action and of the intertextual and interdiscursive relations of texts, in this book I consider borders to be a key topic in the various articulations of the discourse of the nation in the USA. Borders are discussed when talking about the nation in various textual, generic and discursive configurations (e.g. when talking about immigration or the nation's sovereignty and security). Indeed, as a discourse topic, borders are constantly represented in connection with the nation's security and protection. By the same token, borders have also been the recipients of certain recontextualisations of discourse, whereby, through interdiscursivity, other discourses have merged with the traditional roles assigned to borders within the nation. While this book's focus of analysis is the language of political texts, borders as a discourse topic are also part of discourses related to other fields of action, such as diplomacy and foreign policy. Academic disciplines other than Linguistics—Geopolitics, Border Studies or History, for example—have addressed the role of borders in such fields of action. Some influential interpretations of borders proposed by these disciplines will be discussed in the following sections of this chapter. This will be done in order to develop a truly interdisciplinary approach and to provide an interpretation of borders in current US discourse with a wider political and social context.

Borders and the nation: discourses of inclusion and exclusion

The role of borders is constructed and negotiated in discourses about the nation very frequently and at multiple levels. Discourses of the nation address borders as necessary structures of power in the geographical, political and social landscape associated with the idea of the nation. Borders contribute to institutionalise and legitimise the existence of the nation by justifying its sovereignty in a specific territory and within the system of international relations. According to Newman, borders are "the physical and highly visible lines of separation between political, social and economic spaces" (2006: 144), and each nation consists of (and spatially coincides with) one such separated space. The importance of borders in the world of nations has long been established and is connected to the nature of the nation itself: since its birth in the modern sense in the late eighteenth century, the nation has been defined mainly by the territorial domain it coincides with (or, put in another way, by the territory it occupies): "the equation nation = state = people," legitimised the link between nation and territory "since structure and definition of states were now essentially territorial" (Hobsbawm 1992: 19). The meaning of borders is therefore intimately connected to the authority and power exercised by a nation's government: borders originate from the self-imposed spatial-linear limitation of governments and are a delimiting and defining territorial principle for the legally accepted sovereignty of the nation.

A nation's borders communicate an overall impression of stability as well as of simplicity, as if they were fixed and eternal instruments defining the existence of the nation. If viewed in the context of the geography of power in a nation, borders are (peripheral) structures of power wielded by the (central) authority of the nation. A nation is limited by, and included in, its borders, which indicate where each nation ends and another begins. However, the fact that borders are at (and constitute) the geographic margins of a nation does not mean that they have a secondary function. Indeed, the opposite is true: nations use borders as normative entities, as it is through them that both access to the nation and/or nationality are bestowed on individuals. Borders also have the power of discriminating between different communities' social and economic conditions: being on one side or another of a border can mean differences in access to education, health care or economic growth (De Blij 2009), and generally the richest and most powerful nations want to preserve such differences.

Nations exercise their power over borders (and in turn draw power from them) because they are conceptualised and narrated as key elements of the nation within its public sphere. In Benedict Anderson's famous argument, a nation is an "imagined community," in that its members cannot all know each other, but assume, or "imagine," that they are part of a larger community with whom they share certain values making up their national identity. In tracing the main threads of this "imaged community" based on national identity, Anderson notes that one is directly related to the idea of borders: "The nation is imagined as *limited* because even the largest of them, encompassing perhaps a billion living human beings, has finite, if elastic, boundaries, beyond which lie other nations" (Anderson 1991: 7; Anderson's emphasis). Imagining the nation as limited means acknowledging the geographical and institutional space enclosed by borders. The territory of a nation is not just a physical entity: it also has to be *imagined* by the community included in the nation as a self-contained space. As Billig argues, the territorial limitations of a nation as defined by borders is a founding feature of the way a nation is conceived, as "[i]n the *modern nationalist imagination*, one national territory does not shade into another. Nations stop and start abruptly at demarcated borders" (Billig 1995: 74; emphasis mine). Within the discourses of the nation, borders remind people of the finiteness of their own nation, and this aspect inevitably influences how people think of their relationship with the space—both geographical and "imagined"—of the nation and the space outside of it.

The importance of borders at both institutional and "imagined" level should be explained by the way ideologies and power relations *within* the nation are negotiated. Borders are the product of certain historical processes as they are established by a historically determined (and often violent) act of boundary drawing, an act which is in itself one of the clearest displays of a nation's power. However, like all ideological constructs, borders claim naturalness and have become part of a "boundary-consciousness" (Billig 1995: 21) among the nation's members. This consciousness is continually endorsed by institutions of various kinds, such as schools, universities, media and literature, which support "forms of ideological reproduction of the state" (Newman and Paasi 1998: 196) and contribute to the legitimisation of the nation as the natural political division of territory. In this sense, borders are structures of signification which are produced by, but also (re-)produce, the institutional, political and cultural hegemony of the nation over its own territory and population. The naturalisation of borders is part of the naturalising processes associated with the reproduction of the ideology of nationalism. Like other ideologies, nationalism has naturalised all of its basic components, starting from the existence and legitimacy of the nation itself as a form of political organisation, which is perceived as such by the community inhabiting it. The ideological reproduction of borders as part of the nation makes borders a basic cultural and symbolic element— and a particularly powerful one in emotional terms. As Billig argues,

> This world—"our" world—is a place where nations have their official armies, police forces and executioners; where boundaries are rigorously drawn; and where citizens, and male citizens in particular, might expect to be called upon to kill and die in defence of the national border-post.
>
> (1995: 20)

If citizens of a nation, as Billig maintains, "might expect to be called upon to kill and die in defence of the national border-post," there must be strong motivations informing their will, and such motivations cannot be exerted through order, duty or coercion only: they must be made effective through a whole cultural construction and shaped by a set of narratives which legitimise those core elements of national identity, including borders.

Borders play a key role in the ideological legitimisation of the nation as a socio-geopolitical space. They are indeed

> one part of the *discursive landscape* of social power, control and governance, which extends itself into the whole society and which is produced and reproduced in various social and cultural practices. This landscape

concretizes and attempts to legitimize relations between territorial structures.

(Newman and Paasi 1998: 196; emphasis by the authors)

For this reason, borders influence our way of thinking: as Agnew argued,

Borders matter, then, both because they have real effects *and* because they trap thinking about and acting in the world in territorial terms. They not only *limit* movements of things, money, and people, but they also *limit* the exercise of intellect, imagination, and political will.

(2008: 176; emphasis by the author)

In this sense, borders are also "processes" (Anderson 1996: 1–3), in that they are markers of identity which played an essential role in narratives of the nation in making national identity the hegemonic political identity of the twentieth century and continue to do so in the twenty-first century.

In discourses of the nation, borders also act as a discourse topic causing and legitimising either inclusion in, or exclusion from, the nation. This is a typical process associated with the construction of nationalism as an ideology. Nationalism is based on the notion that citizens of a given nation have distinctive features which are unique to their belonging to that nation, and these features separate them from citizens of other nations. In turn, the hegemonic, self-containing and limiting nature of borders within the nation is instrumental in developing the dichotomy between inclusion (for those who are legally resident in the nation or have free access to it) and exclusion (for those who are outside the nation and are either prevented from entering it or subjected to various kinds and degrees of bureaucratic and physical hurdles before entering it). This dichotomy shapes the contours of the various identities associated with (and *created by*) borders and acts as a discriminatory principle on which one's belonging to the nation is founded:

Like the Janus-faced nationalisms with which they are intimately associated in the so-called sovereign nation-state, borders look inwards and outwards: they simultaneously unify and divide, include and exclude. They are coercive, disabling and limiting, including and excluding many people against their will; but they are also benign and enabling, providing the basis for security, dominant forms of identity and conventional representative democracy. "Prison" or "refuge", they can facilitate oppression or provide an escape from it.

(Anderson and O'Dowd 1999: 596)

Thus, borders function as the geopolitical limits of nations and, as such, are also the line separating the people, culture and society *inside* a nation from those *outside* and belonging to other nations. By enacting the logics of inclusion/exclusion, borders draw the separation between "us" and "them" in visual, physical and institutional terms as well as in discourse, as borders provide discourses of nationalism as the ideal line of separation between "our" nation and all other nations. It is nations themselves that are constantly constructed in terms of an opposition between "us," the members of a nation, and "they," those outside the nation (Hobsbawm 1992: 170).

Borders are not just (seemingly) fixed lines of demarcation, even though they give exactly that impression. Borders are territorial and institutional markers of different areas and places, and "it is through and at borders that the specific character of the rigidity and openness of the governance of places becomes most clearly manifested" (van Houtum and van Naerssen 2001: 129). However, borders also "symbolise a *social practice* of spatial differentiation" (van Houtum and van Naerssen 2001: 126; emphasis mine): and they do so, for example, by regulating flows of people, allowing or denying international mobility. Borders do more than that: they play a key role in the definition of the socio-spatial identity connected to the idea of the nation and have a normative nature through which people's social identities are defined. Bordering, that is, the spatial division imposed by the construction and institutionalisation of borders, is strictly related to "othering," a practice of exclusion and marginalisation of those "outside" the borders. It is through bordering and othering that we can construct axiological categories based on the differentiation between "us" and "them," which exemplify the idea of inclusion and exclusion within the nation. In this sense, borders both exclude and include, as they "attempt to create exclusive 'us' identities and, by definition, outsider images of the 'Other'" (Newman and Paasi 1998: 196). Borders not only create (or, we should say, aspire to create) unity and uniformity inside their perimeter (i.e. the nation), but also create and (re) produce differences by keeping the "others" distant spatially and in terms of identity.

The categories of "us" and "them" are not innate in the nation, even though they are presented as if they were, and are established through certain socio-historical processes whereby a certain group becomes hegemonic within the nation and decides the rules of citizenship. The hegemony of a certain group within a nation has been codified by Billig in his "syntax of hegemony," whereby "one part—one aspect of the linguistic and cultural mosaic—will become the dominant, metonymic representation of the whole" (Billig 1995: 87). Billig's notion of the syntax of hegemony derives from Tajfel's Social Identity Theory, which holds that a group constructs its own identity if the members of that group feel that affiliation and commonality through categorisation. Categorisation is thus naturally divisive and exclusive, as self-identification also presupposes a non-identification with all those who do not belong to that group.

Nationalism is based on group categorisations that are the product of a certain hegemonic process, and such categories need to have a certain identity referred to them. As Billig notes, "nationalism is, above all, an ideology of the first person plural" (Billig 1995: 70). When speaking of the nation, people subsume their collective identity in the pronoun "we." This happens very often when a leader of a country speaks by using a "collective we," in which "we" is used as if it embodied the whole nation. Indeed, by defining whom it includes, a nation automatically also indicates those who are excluded from it. The "othering" of groups represented as outside the nation is therefore part of the very nature of a nation. This hegemonic process is exclusive first of all within the nation itself: in most cases, nationalism is "internally exclusive" (Marx 2002: 107) as it marginalises (and in some cases may even expel) certain groups on the basis of some supposed ethnic, linguistic or cultural diversity. The principles used to define membership of the nation and to exclude some groups from it are not just those encoded in law, but are also economic, social, and ethnic, and, crucially, are also embedded in parts of the political or media discourse. Indeed, nations, and the values attributed to (and celebrated by) those who are part of them, do not only have to be *imagined*. They also need to be narrated through different texts and discourses and shared by citizens.

From bordered to borderless—and back: borders, populism and the politics of security (and insecurity)

Despite the apparent stability projected by borders as instruments of nations' legitimisation, their function has changed diachronically and may also differ according to the geopolitical context of the nations they separate. Disruptive changes in the way borders are structured (and, as a consequence, in the projected integrity and stability of the nation) may take place: borders can disappear (e.g. when East and West Germany were reunified in 1990), new borders can be created (as when Yugoslavia fractured in seven different political and national entities in the 1990s), or they can shift and move, changing the territorial extent of a nation (as the Saarland border between France and Germany did during the twentieth century); lastly, existing borders can be made "thinner" or "thicker," that is more or less accessible to "others" seeking to enter the nation. The last 30 years have witnessed an oscillation between border-strengthening and border-weakening, following the evolution of both global and local circumstances and responding to often contradictory socio-political and economic demands.

In the late 1980s, borders seemed to be on the verge of losing much or even all of their functions, both institutionally and culturally. To many observers, the fall of the Berlin Wall in November 1989 heralded a new age in which the function of borders as elements of separation between national spaces would be superfluous. The neoliberal ethics of globalisation, under the impetus of unrestrained, cross-border flows of goods, services, finances and people, and based on the limitless possibilities of a world without barriers, or a "global village," appeared to be increasingly turning nations into obsolete socio-political units. Globalisation in this sense seemed to have replaced a "space of places" with a "space of flows," where boundaries such as national borders were becoming less and less relevant (Castells 1989). Many scholars held that a process of de-territorialisation was taking place, whereby nations would lose their former power of control, including that exercised by borders, whose geopolitical nature would be based on interaction, and not division or separation, between different communities. Writing in 1995, Ohmae argued that "nation states have *already* lost their role as meaningful units of participation in the global economy of today's borderless world" (1995: 11; emphasis in the original). Indeed, borders were seen as "increasingly redundant, and thinking constrained by them restricts thinking about alternative political, social, and economic possibilities" (Agnew 2008: 176). In the globalised world, where boundaries no longer prevent the flows of information and people, the changing socio-spatial organisation has been seen as causing the loss of the relationship between boundaries and territory and, as a consequence, the traditional definitions of identity based on principles of territorial fixity (Newman and Paasi 1998: 192–193). From this perspective, borders have become cultural and social signposts where trans-national and migrant identities are constructed rather than limited or prevented, and a "borderless world" seemed to many quite a realistic prospect.

However, even during the apparent triumph of the "global village" and of a borderless world, borders never really disappeared. The 9/11 terrorist attacks on the Twin Towers and the Pentagon and the financial crisis of 2008 signalled the end of unbridled optimism about the disappearance of borders and the freedom of movement between nations. Open borders were regarded as dangerous for the nation's security: many nations fortified their borders in an effort to fulfil the promise of security to their populations, as the movements of people across borders were increasingly seen (and, crucially, *represented*) as a threat to national security (Diener and Hagen 2009: 1197). Strengthened borders responded to the perceived sense of vulnerability of the entire fabric of civilisation, which was felt to be under attack first because of the threat of terrorism, and more recently of an uncivilised "other" who threatened to disrupt "our" social and economic order (Jones 2012: 12–16).

In many respects, a key year for the progressive tightening of border restrictions and security was 2016. Two political events in that year, that is the Leave victory in the Brexit referendum in the UK and Donald Trump's election as the president of the USA, were unmistakable signs of the continuing power of nationalism and its (cultural, social, political, as well as discursive) paradigm based on the inclusion/exclusion dichotomy. These events were also the clearest evidence yet seen of the appeal that populist parties and leaders had in many countries. Populist politicians, with their highly divisive rhetoric, put border and national security at the centre of the political debate, magnifying the perceived danger to a nation's security posed by the transnational movements of people which had started in the crises of 9/11 and 2008 and continues to this day due to wars, famine and climate crisis in various parts of the world. Against this backdrop, the growing demands for the nation's securitisation led to a reconfiguration of borders, which have progressively become "stronger" and less penetrable (Deleixhe, Dembinska and Iglesias 2019: 643). Faced with globalisation and the erosion of with national sovereignty resulting from the increasing demands of belonging to international organisations and, in some cases, by the renewed threats of devolution at a local, intra-national level, many populist politicians call for (and have sometimes managed to increase) security at national borders, often by building or proposing to militarise borders or to build physical walls to protect the nation. While some argue that the tightening of borders was somehow the swansong of the nation's authority over its own territory (Brown 2010), it seems clear that many populist parties and governments led by populist leaders in many nations have asserted the rule of central power: in many segments of the public sphere, the sovereignty of a nation is seen as deriving from the degree of control it exerts over its territory and borders.

The rise of populism has been seen as a response to the ontological insecurities caused by the rising fear and the sense of (often external) threat felt within society (Steele and Homolar 2019). As theorised by Giddens, ontological security arises from the confidence that people have in their individual and social existences: it is the "[c]onfidence or trust that the natural or social worlds are as they appear to be, including the basic existential parameters of self and social identity" (Giddens 1984: 375). To gain an electoral advantage, populists exploit the sense of uncertainty and anxiety about some threat encroaching upon the security of "ordinary" individuals, the "people" of the nation. According to Inglehart and Norris,

> Anxiety arising from contemporary events—boatloads of migrants and refugees flooding into Europe, images of the aftermath of random acts

of domestic terrorism in Paris, Brussels, and Istanbul, and austerity measures—is blamed for exacerbating economic grievances linked with rising income inequality, the loss of manufacturing jobs, and stagnant wages.

(Inglehart and Norris 2016: 11)

In the populist rhetoric, an external agent or "Other" threatens the nation and its structures and becomes the main cause of the nation's social and economic ills.

The relationship between insecurity and populist politics based on nationalism is so close that it seems that the two cannot really be separated in the current political climate. As a collective phenomenon involving society, insecurity may be defined as a social and political construction: it is "the state of fear or anxiety stemming from a concrete or alleged lack of protection" (Béland 2007: 320), in that it combines the anxiety felt by individuals with their sense of not being adequately protected, and when certain sources of insecurity are collectivised, they become social and political matters. Béland also usefully employs the concept of "threat infrastructure," that is "the nature of the risks that characterize a policy area, and, by extension, the basic political conditions that are likely to stem from such risks" (Béland 2007: 321). Whatever the structural nature of the risk or threat involved—natural or human, occasional or long-lasting—different responses will be generated in the public sphere. Indeed, the infrastructure implies that the threat is made up of both structural and constructed (i.e. not real) components, and the relationship between these two sets of components shapes how the threat itself is perceived. The threat becomes concrete and central in the politics of insecurity only if and when it is framed by the political actors. However, by the same token, "threats have a concrete basis that affects how political leaders mobilize over—and help shape the perception of—these threats" (Béland 2007: 322). It is this infrastructure that helps mould the state's response to the threat in its various possible articulations and sources (the environment, the economy, security), which are both subjective and collective.

Mobilisation over a threat (in the case of border security, the arrival of unwanted foreigners, be they immigrants, refugees or terrorists) and governments' solutions to this threat (e.g. repressive policies on the "aliens" and reinforcement of borders) can only be achieved by constructing such threats socially and discursively and presenting them as dangerously close to the public, and therefore calling for decisive measures. Politicians' construction of a politics of insecurity entails two connected processes: agenda setting and framing. The former consists of selecting the items which become the focus of public attention; in so doing, politicians present themselves as the only ones who can protect the public by solving the issues they present as threats. The latter consists in the simplification—or often over-simplification—of both the threats and the proposals for fighting them. Threats and the sense of insecurity coming with them can be exaggerated, so that the public will be induced to trust the politicians' ability to respond to the threat (Béland 2007: 332–333). Populist leaders and parties have employed the politics of insecurity and have made it one of their main appeals to voters: they propose simple solutions to defend the (supposedly threatened) national unity and integrity from dangers presented by both internal and external enemies and from a sense of impending crisis. In this sense, crisis does not so much cause populism as it is created by it, as populists act in a "performance of crisis" (Moffitt 2016: 114), whereby a crisis is first identified on the basis of some real or exaggerated policy failure, then is played up in media and finally is given simple solutions based on the populist leader's strong leadership. These simple solutions, for example Trump's wall, which would prevent the influx of unwanted foreigners in the USA across the US–Mexico border, both reflect and further radicalise the polarised and simplified political space (the "people" vs the establishment and/or the "Other") typically drawn by populists.

It should be said that the idea of "strong" borders, including the wall proposed by Trump, is not something new or unique to the populist construction of the nation and its emphasis on territorial integrity. Indeed, while borders are usually designated as markers of the nation's sovereignty, originally they often served as military instruments to prevent aggression from neighbouring states. Some modern borders still have an explicitly defensive function and are heavily militarised (e.g. the border between North and South Korea). Many current borders have also morphed into barriers designed to keep unwanted foreigners or outsiders away from the nation (Jones 2012: 9–12). Borders may therefore become "stronger" and less penetrable in order to limit movement. Such borders have been given the name of "fortified boundaries" (Hassner and Wittenberg 2015). The primary function of such boundaries, which are somehow halfway between a militarised border and a conventional demarcation line between two nations, is border control and limitation of movement, and their nature is both physical and asymmetrical. In other words, they are built by one nation to prevent movement of people coming from a neighbouring nation, and their construction is "a one-sided act in response to a unilateral threat, executed without the support (and usually without the consent) of the target state, and often accompanied by protests from the target state" (Hassner and Wittenberg 2015: 162). A "fortified boundary" thus defined is therefore an instrument of power wielded by a nation to prevent people's arrival from the neighbouring nation(s).

The idea behind Trump's wall is by no means new, and is part of an upward trend in the number and length of walls which started, quite paradoxically, at the end of the Cold War, an event which was in fact symbolised by the fall of the Berlin Wall. While by the end of the Cold War there were a mere 12 border walls, the number rose to 45 in 2011, and the surge picked up speed after 9/11. Estimates of the total length of walls worldwide vary, but by 2011 it was estimated to be about 29,000 kilometres (Vallet 2014: 2). Walls make the populist and nationalist programme of exclusion tangible, as images of borders made of walls and fences have become the most visible response to risk and are becoming increasingly important in a nation's security management. In many international contexts, walls have been erected along the borders of nations ostensibly in order to protect them from external enemies. In fact, borders are reinforced by (and to all intents and purposes *become*) walls when governments want to fight a feeling of insecurity in the face of either real, exaggerated or imaginary enemies.

The sense of insecurity and, conversely, the importance of inter- and trans-national security promoted by nationalist and populist movements and made explicit by the growing emphasis on walls can be seen, as argued in the first section of this chapter, as a reaction to the supposed dangers of terrorism or immigration, two categories that often overlap in the discourse of the wall's supporters (Jones 2009), and to the threat of a borderless world, itself the geopolitical basis of globalisation. Running counter to a globalised and cosmopolitan identity and portrayed as a solution to outside dangers, "thickening" borders by means of walls or other measures of protection leads to the "institutionalization of othering" (Konrad 2014: 96). The institutional construction of security has been made visible through walls, fences, heavy militarisation and aggressive document checks, and aims at showing a visible implementation of the differences between nations. The result of increasingly pervasive security can be seen in what happens both in the nations themselves and in borderland communities, which are usually human spaces of social exchange and communication: "[t]his polarization is not conducive to communication or mediation, and, in fact, leads to human distress and trauma, as well as *spatial segregation and place distinction*" (Konrad 2014: 98; emphasis mine).

In discussing the separation of states through walls, and quoting real examples from history (the Great Wall of China, Hadrian's Wall, the Berlin Wall and the wall separating Israel from the Palestinians), Kolossov explains the need to build border walls as a way to isolate, protect and "contain" the nation:

> In the mass consciousness, the perception of external threat gives rise to the aspiration to minimise or to cease all contacts with an undesirable

or dangerous neighbour. If it is impossible to get rid of him, to subordinate, control or resettle him, the best solution will be to build a fence as a protection against him.

(2005: 619)

Of course, walls may be projected or built not because there is necessarily an actual danger from a neighbouring nation or from incoming strangers. Indeed, promoting the construction of a wall may generate (or contribute to generate) a public *impression* of danger, as the prospect of a wall itself evokes the idea of protection from (supposed) external dangers. In fact, a wall can worsen conflicts rather than solve them: paradoxically, while a wall purportedly aims at reassuring a national community and providing them with security, at the same time the appearance of a wall also signals danger and generates inter-state tension. However, walls work within the discourse of nationalism because they communicate the appearance of security in the face of a supposedly impending threat from beyond the borders. As Vallet argues, the decision to build a wall follows a "logic of perception": the optics of a wall or fortified barrier are more important than how effective it would actually be in protecting nations and in addressing the "perceived insecurity" (2014: 3) in their public sphere. Indeed, walls and barriers "restore spectacularly a semblance of control over transnational flows" (Deleixhe, Dembinska and Iglesias 2019: 642) and act as visible, tangible artefacts which project a sense of security in the national consciousness, without actually being totally effective instruments of protection. In fact, it can be said that the most important function of walls and fences is that of creating "facts on the ground," that is visible artefacts of a government's will to put its authority and power on display, quite independently of their effectiveness in stopping the flow of unwanted strangers (Hassner and Wittenberg 2015: 165): the efficacy of a walled or "strong" border as a barrier to unwelcome guests or as a deterrent for border crossing is extremely difficult to assess (Hassner and Wittenberg 2015: 184–187).

Border security and the restrictions on cross-border movements appear to be the new normal, in the USA and elsewhere. This new (or renewed) notion of borders plays well into the exclusive/inclusive nature of a certain kind of nationalism, one based on rigidly drawn boundaries in terms of political, social and cultural identity. The new nationalist scenarios based on polarisation between states and fixed (or often re-fixed) border lines are becoming the distinctive trait of the politics of insecurity. The discourse of modern nationalism evokes and aspires to a form of ethnolinguistic homogeneity which is rooted in the past, a past which in actual fact never truly existed or was not the golden age it is claimed to be. Nationalism is always based on the distinction between "us" and a threatening "them." These categories have found a physical, visible element of separation and discrimination in borders and have been institutionalised through discourse.

2 The Trump Wall

The discourse and the aesthetics of exclusion

The proposal to build a wall on the border between Mexico and the USA was one of Donald Trump's signature campaign promises in his 2016 presidential run and played no small part in his win in that year's general election. The border wall, together with the controversy surrounding its construction, costs and still rather dubious benefits, would become one of the centrepieces of the Trump presidency. For his supporters, the wall was necessary to keep unwanted foreigners out of the USA, while for Trump's detractors, it was the symbol of the President's nativist ideology, divisive policies and hostility to migrants.

The first section of this chapter addresses how the former president used his wall as the basis for constructing narratives of inclusion and exclusion. Specifically, it focuses on the role of borders in Trump's discourse of nationalism and on the way the wall became the core discourse topic of his nativist and "exclusive" idea of the nation. The key motivations for his proposed wall were security and protection from "illegal immigrants" and other supposedly dangerous foreign individuals. At the same time, the border wall was for Trump a necessary prerequisite for the existence of the nation itself. The second and third sections of this chapter analyse the discourse strategies underlying the aesthetics of Trump's border politics, and specifically the presentation of the proposed barrier as a "beautiful wall." Trump constantly highlights his own presence behind the wall he wants to build, a "beautiful wall" which is often described in terms which Trump usually used for luxury properties. This recontextualisation of discourse points to an aesthetic of exclusion, whereby the idea of national belonging and inclusion is expressed in terms of a social privilege to be asserted, and even flaunted, in the face of outsiders. The personalisation of the wall as the "Trump Wall," that is, the association of Trump's name and image with the wall, is so strong that it has become standardised in the USA's political discourse, and the "Trump Wall," along with its variants "Trump's Wall" and "Trump's Border Wall," shows many of the typical aspects of branding. Trump's

DOI: 10.4324/9781003287971-3

frequent own-name-branding of the wall is part of a "name-brand populism" which associates the making of the wall with Trump's name and with all the associated aesthetic implications, in very much the same way as do the other products associated with his name brand (e.g. the Trump Tower).

The border wall: security and the nation

Trump's border policy, and particularly his proposed wall, was perhaps the most distinctive feature of his primary and presidential campaigns and figured prominently throughout his first (and so far, only) mandate, which ran from 2016 to 2020. The idea of building a wall on the USA–Mexico border to prevent the arrival of migrants, criminals and terrorists appeared impractical, controversial or even ridiculous to many, especially among Democratic and progressive-leaning voters. However, Trump's idea garnered plaudits from vast sections of the conservative electorate and helped Trump win first the Republican nomination, and then the Presidential race over his Democratic rival Hillary Clinton.

The issue of the wall certainly did resonate well with the Republican electorate. An August 2015 Rasmussen poll found that 70% of likely Republican voters supported the wall, with 51% of total voters agreeing with the idea (Rasmussen Reports 2015). A poll conducted a month later painted a similar picture: while the American public still seemed generally divided on the issue of the wall (48% opposed it, while 43% were in favour), the figures for each party told a very different story: 73% of Republicans supported the wall, as against only 31% of Democrats (Monmouth University Poll 2015). As of March 2016, the wall remained the single most popular issue regarding immigration among Trump's supporters: 79% of them backed his idea of building a wall, while other immigration issues were much less appealing (Doherty 2016, Gramlich 2016).[1] While Trump's wall and his border policy responded ostensibly to the Republican electorate's worries about immigration, a militarised border was also allegedly aimed at protecting the USA from the dangers posed by foreign terrorists and the globalised economy. As discussed in Chapter 1, globalisation was connected to open borders and liberalised trade, and the prospect of a "fortress USA" could be very appealing to those groups who felt threatened by the arrival of a cheap labour force. In this connection, Trump tapped his base's mood: four months before the November 2016 elections, the top three issues in order of importance for Trump voters were the economy (90%), terrorism (89%) and immigration (79%) (Doherty 2016, Gramlich 2016). Similar percentages were registered just after the elections: at 63.4%, immigration was the third most important issue among Trump voters in 2016—in sharp contrast with the priorities expressed by

Hillary Clinton's supporters—after the size of government (70%) and the budget deficit (64.7%), with terrorism a close fourth at 61.4% (Winston 2017). Thus, it appears that Trump developed his border policy by merging it with immigration and economics policies, both of which were major concerns for most Republicans. Enthusiasm for the wall gradually declined as the Trump administration approached its end: as of January 2019, a majority of the American public (58% to 40%) opposed the expansion of the USA–Mexico border wall (Gramlich 2019). However, the nexus of borders, security and sovereignty was well implanted in US political discourse and, as will be discussed in Chapter 3, would also be part of the notion of borders developed by Democrats.

Trump announced his wall project in June 2015, early in the Republican nomination season, but few know that he had already advanced the idea in his 2011 book, *Time to Get Tough*. In what amounts to an early political manifesto, Trump discussed the 20-foot wall built on the USA–Mexico border in Yuma, Arizona, claiming that this wall was instrumental in reducing the number of illegal immigrants entering the country and arguing that "properly built walls work" (Trump et al. 2011: 147). Other Republicans were no less forthright about the usefulness of building a wall as a barrier to illegal immigration. Conservative pundit Ann Coulter was one of the most influential advocates of restrictive measures for immigration. In her best-selling book *¡Adios America!* (2015), she looked at how Israel and China strengthened their borders (with Palestinian territories and North Korea, respectively) by building fences, preventing the intrusion of unwanted illegal aliens as well as potential terrorists, and advocated the same policy for the USA–Mexico border.[2] Clearly, then, the issue of the wall was explicitly raised in conjunction with that of immigration as well as with that of terrorism. In fact, while in reality they are two separate social categories, in Trump's rhetoric immigrants and terrorists become one group with one single identity.

Trump's first TV ad is an excellent synopsis of the verbal and visual strategies regarding borders and the wall which the then-candidate would employ in the 2016 campaign and beyond. Released on January 4, 2016 (Bevan 2016), the 30-second video highlights the dangers to the USA presented by both Islamic terrorists and immigrants. A photo of Barack Obama and Hillary Clinton (0:02–0:03) was immediately followed by the mugshots of two Muslim terrorists who were responsible for a mass shooting in San Bernardino, California (0:04–0:05), implicitly conflating Islamic terrorists and the Democratic leadership. Trump attacks "Radical Islamic Terrorism," calling for a "temporary ban on Muslims entering U.S." and promising to "cut the head off of ISIS." The images evoking the dangers of terrorism are seamlessly followed by those of a crowd, supposedly immigrants storming a wall, presumably a border wall, with the voiceover suggesting that it was the border between the USA and Mexico, while in reality it was a border wall in Morocco (Emery and Jacobson 2016). The final promise, to stop "illegal immigration," would be fulfilled by "building a wall on the southern border that Mexico will pay for." Terrorists and immigrants are represented as the most dangerous threats to the nation and are merged into one single, undifferentiated group in Trump's ad and in much of his subsequent border rhetoric. Trump's remedy for the risk presented by immigrants and terrorists is the wall, which would prevent these dangerous individuals from entering the USA. Clearly then, Trump's gloomy outlook on the USA saw it as a nation quite literally under siege by foreign enemies, that is, terrorists, immigrants and, during the 2016 Syrian crisis, refugees. All these categories are located by Trump as spatially and morally outside the nation but posing a danger to it.

In Trump's strategy for talking about borders during the Republican primaries, immigrants crossing the USA–Mexico border are constantly referred to as "criminal" and "illegal." As implicit evaluations, these adjectives place immigrants outside the legal and moral norms of society and represent them as a danger to the American nation. "Illegal" was Trump's most frequent label for immigrants. As of May 2021, of the 3182 references to immigration found in Trump's texts on the Factbase website (2021), "illegal" collocates with "immigration" (as in "illegal immigration") 696 times, or almost one in four times. Similarly, out of the 583 times "immigrants" appear, "illegal" collocates with it 422 times, a frequency of 72.3%. Trump made these strategies a trademark of his campaign, for example, in the GOP debate on August 6, 2015:

> If it weren't for me, you wouldn't even be talking about illegal immigration.
>
> (Debate: 1st Republican Presidential Candidate
> Debate—August 6, 2015)

or in a televised campaign ad from January 27, 2016:

> We will build a wall. It will be a great wall. It will do what it's supposed to do. Keep illegal immigrants out.
>
> (Trump 2016a)

There are two predications of "illegal immigrants" or "illegal immigration": (1) Immigrants "come in" illegally, and some of them already have a criminal record, and (2) some or most immigrants will commit crimes while in the USA. In particular, Trump considers immigrants from Mexico and central America to be mainly murderers, rapists or drug traffickers, hence the need to keep them out:

> The military is standing there holding guns and people are just walking right in front, coming into our country (…) You've got these people coming, half of them are criminals.
> (Campaign Speech, Des Moines, IA, January 24, 2016)

> I am extremely, extremely tough on illegal immigration. I'm extremely tough on people coming into this country.
> (Chris Wallace Interviews Donald Trump on
> Fox News Sunday—October 18, 2015)

> We have to stop the inflow of illegals coming into our country.
> (Trump 2016a)

The correlation of immigration and crime is then shored up by Trump's use of official data. A section of his programme published online in August 2015 called "Immigration Reform that will Make America Great Again" mentions two instances of crime, supported by media reports and statistics:

> The impact [of illegal immigration from Mexico] in terms of crime has been tragic. In recent weeks, the headlines have been covered with cases of criminals who crossed our border illegally only to go on to commit horrific crimes against Americans. Most recently, an illegal immigrant from Mexico, with a long arrest record, is charged with breaking into a 64 year-old woman's home, crushing her skull and eye sockets with a hammer, raping her, and murdering her. The Police Chief in Santa Maria says the "blood trail" leads straight to Washington. In 2011, the Government Accountability Office found that there were a shocking 3 million arrests attached to the incarcerated alien population, including tens of thousands of violent beatings, rapes and murders.
> (Trump 2015b)

By mentioning official figures and news items, Trump wanted to provide his audience with empirical evidence of the danger posed by illegal immigrants as a whole. The inclusion of official data from government offices ("a shocking 3 million arrests attached to the incarcerated alien population") follows the so-called number game (van Dijk 2000, 2005), a discourse strategy whereby official figures communicate objectivity, thus lending credibility to Trump's discourse and the danger he projects onto immigrants.

In his discourse on immigrants and immigration during his presidential campaign, Trump evoked two other groups of social actors, Muslim terrorists and refugees, and specifically refugees from Syria, often citing them in connection with illegal immigration. In Trump's interview with Fox on October 18, 2015, he was asked about the 9/11 terrorist attacks and what he would have done to prevent them had he been president at the time. In his answer, Trump related terrorism to illegal immigration:

> Well, I would have been much different, I must tell you. Somebody said, well, it wouldn't have been any different. Well, it would have been. I am extremely, extremely tough on illegal immigration. I'm extremely tough on people coming into this country. I believe that if I were running things, I doubt those families would have—I doubt that those people would have been in the country. So there's a good chance that those people would not have been in our country.
> (Chris Wallace Interviews Donald Trump on Fox News Sunday, October 18, 2015)

Trump continually emphasises the notion of poor security at the US borders and advocates being "extremely tough on illegal immigration" and "on people coming into this country." The notion of illegal immigrants merges with that of terrorists and Syrian refugees in many of his speeches. In Des Moines, Iowa, on January 24, 2016, Trump uses the same categories of predication for Syrian refugees, terrorists and illegal immigrants, as they all come across the border illegally to threaten the USA:

> They're walking. The military is standing there holding guns and people are just walking right in front, coming into our country. It is so terrible. It is so unfair. It is so incompetent. And we don't have the best coming in. We have people that are criminals, we have people that are crooks. You can certainly have terrorists. You can certainly have Islamic terrorists. You can have anything coming across the border. We don't do anything about it.
> (Campaign Speech, Des Moines, IA, January 24, 2016)

The distance between immigrants and US citizens implied in Trump's discourse through certain instances of nomination and predication is reinforced by the use of *they*. In attacking immigrants, Trump uses the third person plural pronoun as part of his negative representation of all (potential or actual) enemies of America. The plural pronoun does not always identify a specific and recognisable group of individuals, but rather, for example, undifferentiated, generalised Mexicans who are given negative nominations and predications. As Trump declared on June 16, 2015, in the speech announcing his presidential bid:

> When Mexico sends its people, they're not sending their best. They're not sending you. They're not sending you. They're sending people that have lots of problems, and they're bringing those problems with us. They're bringing drugs. They're bringing crime. They're rapists. And some, I assume, are good people.
>
> (Speech: Donald Trump Announces His Candidacy in
> New York, NY, June 16, 2015)

In this quotation, the identity of *they* switches from a collectivised Mexico as a nation ("they're not sending their best. They're not sending you. They're not sending you. They're sending people that have lots of problems") to immigrants themselves ("and they're bringing those problems with us. They're bringing drugs. They're bringing crime. They're rapists"), thus attacking at the same time Mexico as a nation and those Mexicans who cross the border. In Trump's text, *they* indicates distance from the "deictic centre" in discourse and points to exclusion, separation and geographical and moral distance from Self, the speaker and his/her audience (Chilton 2004: 57–61). *They* is related to certain material processes ("bringing problems with us," "bring drugs," "bring crime") and relational processes of identification ("They're rapists") which highlight the vicious nature of the "stranger," while the final disclaimer ("And some, I assume, are good people") is too marginal and hedged ("I assume") to defuse the violent rhetoric of Trump's discourse.

Trump made the connection between the wall, secure borders and terrorism very explicitly in his own book *Crippled America*:

> Walls work. The Israelis spent $2 million per kilometer to build a wall—which has been hugely successful in stopping terrorists from getting into the country. (…) While obviously we don't face the same level of terrorist threat as our closest Middle East ally, there is no question about the value of a wall in the fight against terrorism.
>
> (Trump 2015a: 24)

Trump made this connection even more explicit in a Facebook post from November 22, 2015. The post includes a composite of two photos (Figure 2.1). The top photo shows the wall between Israel and the Palestinian territories, while the bottom photo, showing a barbed wire fence, is meant to represent the USA–Mexico border. The post read:

Figure 2.1 Donald J. Trump's Facebook post, November 25, 2015.

> Syrian refugees were caught trying to get into the U.S. through the Southern Border. How many made it? WE NEED THE WALL!
>
> (Trump 2015d)

Trump wrote in response to the news of the arrival in the USA of 13 Syrians, who had crossed the USA–Mexico border, the same border used by "illegal immigrants" from Mexico. Trump highlights the porous nature of the southern border, which is now crossed by people coming from places usually associated with Islamic terrorism. The two stacked photos of the post show a contrast between security (the wall defending Israeli territories from the Palestinian ones) and vulnerability (the weak fences between Mexico and the USA). The assumption is that the Israeli–Palestinian wall is working well and keeps terrorists away, while there is basically no barrier between the USA and Mexico, and the USA is therefore vulnerable and open to attacks from rapists, thieves and terrorists arriving from abroad. By showing the photos of the two borders, Trump is appealing to certain intertextual and interdiscursive features and to the fact that most people in the US side with Israel and associate Palestinians with terrorism. The Israeli wall leads Trump's electorate to interpret the USA–Mexico border as a category of risk similar to that of terrorism, with the wall being the discourse

Figure 2.2 Former President Donald J. Trump and (right) Rodney Scott, chief US Border Patrol agent for San Diego, near one of the wall prototypes, San Diego, March 13, 2018 (Reuters).

topic shared by the two discourses, at the same time reinforcing the issue of security against immigration and terrorism.

The notions of security and danger foregrounded by the discursive construction of the border wall are strengthened by the visual representations of Trump's visit to the border on March 13, 2018. Photos from that visit show Rodney Scott, the Border Patrol's San Diego sector chief, next to Trump (Figure 2.2). Whether or not this was a deliberate choice, the fact that Scott is a white male plays well into the whole nativist framework and the white majority law-and-order mantra to which Trump constantly appeals.

The sense of threat from "outsiders" such as immigrants is reinforced by Trump's use of certain metaphors. According to the discourse strategies identified by the DHA, metaphors can be considered as part of predication in that they lend certain emotional and moral values to the social actors involved. Trump often uses the "flood" metaphor when referring to immigrants or terrorists threatening to cross the southern border into the USA:

> The first thing we need to do is secure our southern border—and we need to do it now. We have to stop that flood, and the best way to do that is to build a wall.

> (Trump 2015a: 23)

We have to stop the inflow of illegals coming in to our country.

(Trump 2016a)

Pew polling shows 83 percent of all voters—Democrats, Republicans and Independents—think immigration should be frozen or reduced. The biggest beneficiaries of allowing fewer foreign workers into our country would be minority workers, including all immigrants now living here, who are competing for jobs, benefits and community resources against record waves of foreign workers.

(Trump 2016b)

The fact is, since then, many killings, murders, crime, drugs are pouring across the border, our money going out and the drugs coming in.

(Debate: 1st Republican Presidential Candidate
Debate, August 6, 2015)

By associating immigrants with a source domain with such sinister implications, Trump implies that their entrance into the nation is akin to a natural catastrophe, thus directing his supporters' moral judgement. The metaphorical image of immigration as a flood or an inundation threatening to disrupt a nation's order has been routinely used in discourses about (and against) immigration (Hart 2010: 153–154) and is well established in right-wing discourse both in the UK and the USA (Charteris-Black 2006; Semino 2008: 95–97). Its ideological implication is to dehumanise immigrants and to deprive them of individual identity (Santa Ana 1999).

There is empirical evidence that the metaphorical use of flood or inundation to characterise immigration as a threat can be very persuasive in political communication and cognition. Through this kind of metaphor, the proposed wall can become particularly effective precisely because of the cognitive link that the metaphor establishes between immigration and a concrete phenomenon such as flooding. The presence of the wall in discourse would make the flood metaphor particularly convincing, as a wall cognitively and even visually stops a flood (Jimenez et al. 2021).

At the level of discourse macrostructures, Trump supports the wall as a discourse topic through the use of argumentative schemes which justify the exclusion of "illegal immigrants" and call for wall-building (Demata 2017). Applying Wodak's argumentation theory, we can identify a *topos* of cause, whereby an argument or cause (i.e. open borders) is followed by an effect or effects (i.e. crime and loss of US jobs). The effects in turn become an argument or *topos* of threat or danger, which must be countered by doing something (i.e. building a wall):

Argument: Our borders are open.
Conclusion rule: Illegal Mexican immigrants who come to the US steal our jobs and commit crimes because our borders are open.
Truth claim: Illegal Mexican immigrants who come to the US steal our jobs and commit crimes.

Argument: Illegal Mexican immigrants who come to the US steal our jobs and commit crimes.
Conclusion rule: If we build a wall, illegal immigrants from Mexico will be stopped.
Truth claim: Illegal immigrants from Mexico will be stopped.

These two *topoi* constitute Trump's preferred structure when talking about the need to build a wall. Trump would restructure or expand the argumentative schemes according to whatever events and circumstances were taking place. For example, in late 2015 he added Islamic terrorists to the dangers facing the USA after the November 13, 2015, attacks in Paris, the San Bernardino shootings in early December 2015, which involved a Muslim couple, and the news of the atrocities committed by ISIS. The two *topoi* of cause and of threat of danger which argued for the wall were thus expanded:

Argument: Our borders are open.
Conclusion rule: Illegal Mexican immigrants *and Islamic terrorists* who come to the US commit crimes because our borders are open.
Truth claim: Illegal Mexican immigrants *and Islamic terrorists* who come to the US commit crimes.

Argument: Illegal Mexican immigrants *and Islamic terrorists* who come to the US commit crimes.
Conclusion rule: If we build a wall, illegal immigrants from Mexico *and Islamic terrorists* will be stopped.
Truth claim: Illegal immigrants from Mexico *and Islamic terrorists* will be stopped.

Clearly, then, a fortified border is justified because of the dangers from those groups who are geographically and socially outside the nation. However, it is the fortified border or wall that draws the line between insiders and outsiders, as it is construed in discourse as a discriminating element in terms of the identity bestowed (or denied) by the nation: a border is a state institution which has the power to regulate access to the motherland but is also construed as a discriminating structure, separating "legal" from "illegal" individuals. Furthermore, borders are also constructed in discourse as key elements of the nation as a legal and social entity. An example of this is a famous interview during CBS' comedy programme "The Late Show with Stephen Colbert," aired on September 22, 2015, when Trump said that he would build a wall with "a beautiful big fat door," by which he meant a legally established entrance to the nation, whereby "people can come into the country, but they have to come in legally. That's what a country is all about." (Trump 2015c)

The lack of border security and integrity becomes part of narratives of insecurity and danger associated with "aliens" who threaten to cross the border. This can be seen in Trump's frequent connection between illegal immigration, borders and the existence of the nation. In the three "core principles of real immigration reform," which are part of "Immigration Reform That Will Make America Great Again," the section on immigration of his manifesto for the 2016 presidential election, Trump addresses the supposedly failed policies on immigration and sees them as an existential threat to the USA:

1. A nation without borders is not a nation. There must be a wall across the southern border.
2. A nation without laws is not a nation. Laws passed in accordance with our Constitutional system of government must be enforced.
3. A nation that does not serve its own citizens is not a nation. Any immigration plan must improve jobs, wages and security for all Americans.

(Trump 2015b)

In Trump's formulation, borders both construct the nation institutionally and produce national identity and difference. The existence of the nation is linked to that of the border, or rather the wall, while at the same time the identity of the individuals outside the border is measured against the laws of the country. Trump would emphasise this identification of borders and nation over and over again:

> Look, we have a country, we have borders. We have no border right now; we don't have a country (...) We can have a great and beautiful wall. When it will be up, it will stop. We'll have our border. And guess what? Nobody comes in unless they have their papers, and they come in legally. And we stop crime, and we stop problems, and we stop drug trade which is massive. You know, we have so much drug trade, the cartels, are pouring through, just like there's nothing, pouring through ... Chicago, New York, Los Angeles ... the money goes out, the drugs come in ... we're gonna stop it.
>
> (Trump 2015c)

We don't have a country if we don't have borders. We will build a wall. It will be a great wall. It will do what it's supposed to do. Keep illegal immigrants out.

(Trump 2016a)

Trump clearly assumes that a nation is such only if and when its border works in preventing the arrival of immigrants from outside the nation. Thus, the border wall has an alienising function that is aimed at reassuring the public and answering their need for security, as the existence of the nation itself is represented as under threat.

The wall proposed by Trump is in line with the concept of fortified border, as a visual (and not necessarily effective) instrument of security for the nation. It also seeks to strengthen the sense of exclusivity in people's belonging to the nation. However, the border wall as envisioned by Trump functions as an instrument of physical and social exclusion not just because of its alienising powers, but also because of the aesthetic values associated with it and constructed in discourse by Trump.

The beautiful wall: borders and the discourse of real estate

The wall never disappeared from public debate during the four years of Trump's presidency, as Trump often found himself struggling to fund its construction and facing stark opposition from Congress and from humanitarian and environmental groups. Yet, as early as his 2016 presidential campaign, the border wall turned from a simple, albeit controversial, proposal to a trademark of Trump's presidency. While Trump often talks about "a" wall or "the" wall, the barrier between Mexico and the USA is often called the "Trump Wall." There is even a Wikipedia entry on the "Trump Wall," an early version of which started with this statement: "The Trump Wall, commonly referred to as 'The Wall', is a colloquial name for a proposed expansion of the Mexico-United States barrier during the U.S. presidency of Donald Trump" (Wikipedia 2020). The fact that the "Trump Wall" is considered a "colloquial name" for Trump's project for a fortified border says a lot about the extent to which the appellative has been circulating in the public sphere: together with its variants "Trump's Wall" and "Trump's Border Wall," the "Trump Wall" has effectively become a key signifier in Trump's nationalism and its discursive articulation around borders.

Trump started mentioning the border wall as his own "Trump Wall" in August 2015, during the Republican presidential primaries. The larger textual context in which Trump's mentions of the wall occur is crucial to understanding the ideological motivations behind his proposal, which does not appeal just to concerns about immigration or terrorism:

> But the reason is we have a message and the message is and essentially we're not gonna take it anymore. We're just not gonna take it anymore. So a couple of weeks ago we came out with our immigration plan. And it's honestly been met with -- I know you've heard, you know, very controversial no. But generally speaking, it's been met with tremendous applause. People are tired of what's happening and part of the plan is the wall. And I was criticized, you can't build a wall. How can you -- you're right. She's obviously in the building real estate business, right? Stand up. Are you in the real estate business? And you know what -- can Trump build a wall? And it's gonna be so beautiful. Because someday when I'm no longer around, they'll call it the Trump Wall. It's got to be the greatest wall. Gotta be the greatest. (...) do you ever see plank that's laid like for highways where they cross highways. It's concrete plank. It's precast. I'm so good at this. That's actually the thing I'm best at. Hey, is that good to have a president that's really good at construction when we have to build our country, rebuild it, our infrastructure?
>
> (Greenville, SC, August 27, 2015)

> But they are coming in with hundreds of -- you have to see this. The numbers they're staggering. Get shipped all over the United States and then people say, oh, the wall doesn't work. You ask Israel whether or not a wall works. Believe me. A wall properly done, a Trump Wall, a Trump Wall works. That I can tell you. (...) You know they say it's going to cost ten or 12 [billion dollars], but that's for people that never built anything. These are people that have no idea. You'll do it for much less, the difference is that it will be bigger and better and stronger. And people aren't going to Home Depot and buying a ladder and walking right over this -- not this wall, not this wall. And by the way, and by the way, this wall is going to have a big beautiful open gate. We're going to have a nice opening. (...) See that's what's going to happen. That's why I'm going to make this wall so beautiful because when I'm gone they're going to probably change the name to the Trump Wall. I've got to make it beautiful. I've got to. Big, big and powerful and beautiful.
>
> (Rochester, NH, September 17, 2015)

> But you have some very bad people. You take a look at some of the gangs in L.A., rough gangs, these are rough dudes. If I get elected, if I become president those people are out of here, those guys are gone, and fast. I mean gone. They are coming back and we're going to put them where

they came from. We're not going to put them in our prisons and take care of them for 45 years. Not going to happen that way. It's not going to happen that way. So they are gone. And we are going to build a wall, and it is going to be a real wall. It's not one of these little walls where they ride jeeps over the top loaded up with drugs, and screw up our cities and the lives of our children and everybody else. There's going to be a real wall. It's going to be a Trump wall. OK? It's going to be a real wall, I know how to do it, believe me. You know something I never talk about, OPO, the old post office, a great building in Washington D.C. In between -- exactly in between the White House and the Capitol, on Pennsylvania Avenue. I am building it. Everybody wanted that building. I got it. In the Obama administration, can you believe it? The most sought after property probably in the history of GSA, everybody. Every hotel company wanted it, Waldorf Astoria, everybody, all the hotel companies. Hyatt wanted it. Pritzker is the biggest backer of Obama. They wanted it. (...) I already have the greatest hotel in America. It is in Chicago. But the greatest hotel in America, it's going to be something that's going to make a lot of people proud. But I know how to build. And that wall is going to be a real wall. And that is going to be a really powerful wall. And it's going to be a beautiful wall, because someday they will probably name it after Trump. [Applause] It has got to be beautiful, it's true; the Trump Wall. It will be called to Trump Wall. And it is going to have a door in it, a big beautiful door, because people are going to come into the country because I want them to, and so do you. But they have got to come in legally.

(Orlando, FL, November 13, 2015)

And I wanted to you know we to be talking about the wall because we're going to build a wall. It's going to be a big wall and it's gonna look beautiful because someday they'll probably end up naming it the Trump Wall. It's got to look beautiful. And people will come through the openings in that wall and we'll have a few of them and they'll come in and they're going to come in legally and to our country.

(Beaumont, TX, November 14, 2015)

You know how easy that is beautiful brick cast concrete going up? I'll tell you one thing if anybody gets to the top of the Trump Wall, it's gonna be a long way down. It's gonna be very scary. It's gonna be a real wall. But they said, you can't really build a wall. And I said about the Great Wall of China, which is very serious wall by the way. I told him about the Great Wall of China. I said look, over there, you're talking about 12,000, 13,000. Over here, you're talking about really a thousand miles, it's 2,000 but -- because I have a lot of natural barriers, etc. They said, you'll never be able to build. It's so easy. So easy. When I can build 6,000 units in the middle of Manhattan on the Hudson River. I can guarantee you. I can guarantee you this is easy by comparison.

(Buffalo, NY, April 18, 2016)

In the above quotations, Trump's descriptions of the wall ("my wall" or "Trump Wall") refer to three different discursive contexts. First, the wall is beneficial because it will reduce immigration and criminality. As seen in the previous section of this chapter, the wall is conceived as a visible and tangible barrier which will prevent or discourage the arrival of unwanted foreigners and protect US citizens. Second, the wall is meant to protect the US economy and jobs from the arrival of a cheap work force. Finally, the wall is discussed in the context of Trump's reputation and supposed prowess as a real estate developer. Building a border wall is compared to building a luxury hotel, where Trump's expertise with the latter is used to prove his ability to build the former. The wall project is discussed in the same context as leasing "the OPO, the old post office, a great building in Washington D.C.," for which he claims he beat the competition from Hyatt and Waldorf Astoria, or "6,000 units in the middle of Manhattan on the Hudson River," all ventures his name brand is famous for. The wall is, in this third discursive context, always described as "beautiful," thus imbuing a state institution with certain aesthetic qualities that Trump borrowed from the discourse of real estate and used as evaluative parameters.

In his political discourse, Trump uses aesthetic attributions very often, not just with reference to the wall. "Beautiful" is in fact one of Trump's most frequently used words, and he has applied it to a wide range of objects, from coal to health care bills, from sleeping gas to US tax dollars, and from Confederate statues to factories built by Apple (Hunston 2017; Todd 2017), often drawing ridicule from media pundits and political observers (e.g. Besanvalle 2020). However, when Trump discusses the border wall in the context of his real estate ventures, the use of words such as "beautiful" is particularly remarkable: the term is shared by the two discourse domains, as it resonates with the language that Trump usually uses when talking about real estate. In his first book, co-authored with Tony Schwartz,[3] *Trump: The Art of the Deal*, "beautiful" is used 39 times, including 8 times referring to women and 23 times to estates, house accessories or views from the properties he had just purchased, was about to sell or belonged to wealthy people, as in, for example:

For what [the upkeep of the Mar-a-Lago residence] costs each year, you could buy a beautiful home almost anywhere else in America.

(Trump and Schwartz 1987: 26)

The first thing we did [in Swifton Village, Cincinnati] was invest in beautiful white shutters for the windows. (...). The next thing we did was rip out the cheap, horrible, aluminum front doors on the apartments and put up beautiful colonial white doors.

(Trump and Schwartz 1987: 84)

And on the avenues, especially Central Park West and Riverside Drive, there were beautiful old buildings with huge apartments and spectacular views. It was only a matter of time before people discovered the value.

(Trump and Schwartz 1987: 107)

Koch has a very nice three-room rent-controlled apartment with a terrace in a beautiful part of Greenwich Village.

(Trump and Schwartz 1987: 255)

This use of "beautiful" (as well as the noun "beauty" and the adverb "beautifully") appears in Trump's other books as well. In *Trump: How to Get Rich*, co-written with Meredith McIver and published in 2004, he speaks of "Sixteen beautifully designed buildings on the Hudson River" when he refers to Trump Place (Trump and McIver 2004: 43), his skyscraper at 40 Wall Street is "the most beautiful building in lower Manhattan" (Trump and McIver 2004: 125), and Trump International Golf Club in Palm Beach, Florida, is home to "the most beautiful golf courses possible" (Trump and McIver 2004: 50). By using "beautiful" in his descriptions of houses and other luxury properties, Trump offers certain aesthetic and emotional connotations linked to locations, facilities and objects denoting high social status and expectations: there is a high social value attached to those things he likes exactly because they are "beautiful." Indeed, the term is also typical of real estate marketing and is very often used in promoting property: as an adjective, "beautiful" is "unambiguously emotive" (Pryce and Oates 2008: 328) and evokes the pathos used as part of the rhetoric employed in real estate marketing, as it taps into the emotional implications of house-buying.

The aestheticisation of Trump's border wall and its connection to the world of real estate and luxury homes may also be observed from a May 2019 report that Trump complained that the planned wall was "ugly" and ordered that it be painted black, so that it would be more beautiful and would at the same time absorb heat, especially during the summer, in order to make it very difficult for migrants to climb (Miroff and Dawsey 2019). Commenting on Trump's remarks on beautifying the wall with paint, David Lapan, a former official at the Department of Homeland Security, claimed that Trump saw himself as "a builder," adding: "But building high-rises in New York City is not the same as putting up a barrier at the border (...) You're not looking for aesthetics, you're looking for functionality" (Miroff and Dawsey 2019). Trump also insisted on calling the bollards "slats," like the wooden strips in a picket fence. Trump had already used the term "slat" in a tweet dated December 18, 2018, when he wrote: "The Democrats are saying loud and clear that they do not want to build a Concrete Wall—but we are not building a Concrete Wall, we are building artistically designed steel slats, so that you can easily see through it ...," and in a speech on the following day he also used the alternative definition of "steel slats." The "artistically designed steel slats," while probably meant to make fun of the Democrats' opposition to the wall, resonate with Trump's own aesthetic vision of building ventures. On December 21, 2018, Trump expanded on the "steel slats" definition, tweeting "A design of our Steel Slat Barrier which is totally effective while at the same time beautiful," with a sketch of the wall, with spikes at the top of the barrier magnified in a small illustration (Figure 2.3). The functionality of the wall in terms of border security ("effective") is therefore nested alongside a logic of aesthetics ("beautiful"), a pairing that would not be out of place in the discourse of a real estate developer or marketer.

Trump's use of "beautiful" taps an aesthetics of pleasure which is commonly attached to a luxury house or a brand product, conferring a certain status on its owner. Given Trump's prominence and role, the status of the wall as beautiful is projected onto the whole nation: being American becomes a privilege, and the "beautiful wall" solidifies this privilege in the eyes of both insiders and outsiders. In his own discourse of the nation, Trump points to a discourse based on the aesthetics of appearance, where style dominates over substance, and which is linked to Trump's own image and lifestyle. Trump conceptualises the wall as more than a border wall, as it has to *appear* in a certain way, over and above its function as a barrier which would supposedly protect the USA from "illegal immigrants" by strengthening an official line of division between nations: calling a border wall "beautiful," providing it with "artistically designed steel slats" and having it painted black because it was "ugly" are not statements that would normally be applied to a border barrier. Trump is here recontextualising the discourse of real estate developers and marketing to the arena of politics and international relations—an arena which, in many respects, is in itself subject to market forces. The use of certain symbols and tropes is connected to a particular, privileged lifestyle, one expressing a certain identity: in

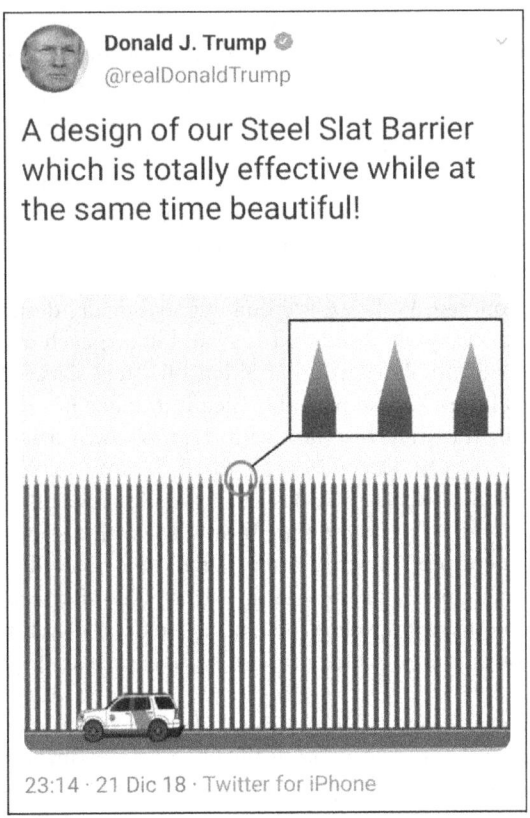

Figure 2.3 Donald J. Trump's tweet, @realDonaldTrump, December 21, 2018.

today's market-dominated society, identities and lifestyles are reified in certain material goods and services (Lorenzo-Dus 2006: 744), and this is what takes place with Trump's aestheticisation of his *beautiful* wall—a border transformed into an object bearing his own brand.

Branding Trump and the Trump Wall

As discussed at the start of the previous section of this chapter, Trump's aestheticisation of the wall is continually associated in discourse with Trump's own name. The Trump Wall is not an official trademark like Trump's commercial products, but it has nevertheless become part of Trump's image. Through Trump's association with "his" beautiful wall and his parallels between the wall and his own business ventures, the Trump Wall presents many of the qualities commonly associated with brands and branding and is somehow connected with the pre-existing Trump brand. Trump himself mentioned the Trump Wall in 15 of his speeches between August 2015 and July 2016 and in one TV interview on November 11, 2015, that is, during his primary and presidential campaigns, but never in later speeches or interviews. Once elected, though the border wall became the core of his immigration and crime policies, he only mentioned the Trump Wall in two tweets. Clearly, Trump was keen to associate his own brand name with the wall very early in his political run so that audiences could immediately recognise it as part of his brand.

The American Marketing Association defines a brand as "a name, term, design, symbol or any other feature that identifies one seller's goods or service as distinct from those of other sellers" (AMA 2020). A brand, though, works because of the associations it creates in the minds of customers: according to the ISO brand standards, a brand "is an intangible asset" that is intended to create "distinctive images and associations in the minds of stakeholders, thereby generating economic benefit/values" (AMA 2020). The importance of these "distinctive images and associations" attached to the brand in connection with (as well as "generating") the actual material or monetary value of the branded object points to the notion that a brand is not just a product: rather, while a product is a tangible object, it also has intangible values and attributes which are created by its being branded. In fact, the power of branding is such that "the right brand can surpass the actual product as the company's central asset" (van Ham 2001: 3). Thanks to branding, the "brand essence" leads to the development of certain "core values" which define the meaning that the brand has among customers, and these values are even more important than the product itself. Stories are created around these core values, and these stories, involving myths and metaphors, lure customers to the brand itself (Flowerdew 2004: 584; Mitsikopoulou 2008: 354). Indeed, a brand "adds an emotional dimension to the products with which people can identify" (Mitsikopoulou 2008: 355), and this emotional dimension is crucial in the customers' involvement with a brand.

Branding also (and crucially) aspires to connect the branded product with certain emotions and "aspirational lifestyles" (Van Gelder 2002) which go beyond the value or the usefulness of the product itself. A key component of the emotional drive of brands as well as of their "saleability" on the market is name-branding. Brand names are very useful as they help a certain product be recognised, but they also embody a set of meanings and symbols which immediately recall the products they are attached to (Levy 1978). Brand names are generally used because of their power in evoking certain associations in the minds of customers, as a well-chosen brand name "can enhance brand awareness and/or help create a favorable brand image for a newly introduced product" (Keller, Heckler and Houston 1998: 48). Brand names are chosen because they "are inherently memorable and therefore facilitate recall and/or recognition in purchase and/or consumption settings," and/or because their "inherent meanings enhance the formation of strong, favorable, and unique brand associations consistent with that meaning" (Keller, Heckler and Houston 1998: 49). A brand name can also be "suggestive" in that it conveys certain attributes or associations. Indeed, choosing a specifically suggestive brand name can be very helpful in inducing customers to remember that brand and all its associated values.

Branding processes should be considered a "semiotic activity" (Lischinsky 2018), as they turn material products into semiotic ones (Mitsikopoulou 2008: 356): certain symbols, languages and images are created and their meaning made available through interaction with "stakeholders." Branding is thus negotiated in discourse: given the importance of brands both in labelling a product and in terms of images and emotional associations among consumers, branding is also a process made up of a set of discursive practices *creating* the symbolic, intangible dimension of brands. Branding infuses objects with their symbolic value, and this can only be done by employing certain discursive strategies. As Flowerdew argues,

> branding is essentially concerned with discursive processes. These discursive processes, developing from the linguistically defined core values, are directed towards the creation (semiosis) of an image or set of images, along with a logo that will define the brand. The purpose of this semiotic process is social action, to persuade people to buy the product or service represented by the brand.
>
> (Flowerdew 2004: 585)

It is through discourse that certain elements of a brand are foregrounded and others hidden or marginalised. Potentially, then, branding is an open-ended process, whereby the meanings attached to the brand via certain discursive strategies can be constantly reformulated and applied to different "objects" and according to different contexts. In this sense, the brand acts as a "'floating' signifier" which is continually recontextualised and reformulated rather than having a fixed identity or meaning (Lischinsky 2018). It is also through discourse that the brand ultimately reaches its goal, that is, of persuading customers to buy the products associated with it. Given that brand management controls the meanings that have to be foregrounded or excluded in the brand, the brand itself has the power to spread these meanings and thus exert the way the brand is known in society (Flowerdew 2004: 585).

Branding is not just an activity that supports companies or corporations. Products and services of many kinds, and even cities or whole nations, are often identifiable (and are structured) as brands (van Ham 2001, 2002). Politics has also long witnessed marketing and branding strategies attached to both political parties and individual politicians, as part of the development of a consumer model of political communication (Scammell 2007). In this sense, branded politicians and parties are one key example of that process of recontextualised discourse (i.e. discourse reconceptualised from marketing to other fields, such as politics) which is a typical component of modern-day branding (Mitsikopoulou 2008: 356–357). Political parties and politicians need branding to make their "product" a desirable commodity in the eyes of the voters/customers. Politics is increasingly seen as a field in which certain principles typical of marketing can be applied. Political campaigns use common marketing strategies (as voters are addressed as if they were customers) and advertising agencies work on and with both products and politicians, often using similar, or even the same, marketing techniques, the difference being that politicians typically "sell" symbolic, abstract and intangible products (O'Shaughnessy 2001). Individual politicians can also be branded and become brand names, as certain features of their personality and/or appearance become a distinctive trait which can be recognised and appreciated by voters. In this sense, the presentation of politicians as brand names can act as a strong incentive to motivate voters. Many politicians in the last 50 years or so have been branded, some notable cases being Tony Blair, whose "New Labour" was rebranded as a totally new and appealing political entity in stark opposition to the "old Labour" and its socialist values (White and De Chernatony 2002; Scammell 2007), and Barack Obama, whose signature "master narrative" merging progressive values and the "American Dream" was sold successfully in two US presidential elections (Conoscenti 2011).

Unlike other politicians who have become successful brands, Trump—or rather, his name—was already a world-famous brand before entering politics. Writing while Trump was still running for the Republican presidential nomination in 2015, branding consultant Nancy Friedman caught the uniqueness of having a would-be President with an already recognisable brand name and listed him as a candidate for the Brand Name of the Year for 2015:

> Yes, Donald J. Trump is a contender for the Republican presidential nomination in 2016. But his name is also used commercially in myriad contexts, extant and defunct—from The Trump Organization

(the real-estate business he inherited) to the Trump World Tower, Trump Restaurants, Trump Productions, Trump Golf, and Trump Chocolate—which makes him the first presidential candidate to also be a brand name.

(Friedman 2015)

As Friedman realised, the image of Trump the tycoon could not be separated from that of Trump the President of the United States of America, and they merged into one single brand and one single brand name. Trump's actions and words did nothing to separate the two identities of his own persona. In fact, he did just the opposite, as he has continually indexed his political actions with the brand identity which was already firmly established and effectively name-branded himself and, in the specific case of the border, the Trump Wall.[4]

As discussed earlier, one of the founding features of branding is the emotional involvement communicated by the brand to its customers. As a "product," the "value" of the Trump Wall is judged on the basis of its effectiveness in stopping immigration, but the emotions associated with the wall and the constant recontextualising of Trump's business discourse into the discourse of borders make branding even more relevant in discussing the Trump Wall. In a political and transnational context in which even nations are increasingly branded, the branding of the Trump Wall is structured according to one of the key factors connected to the way nations are branded: politicians who decide to brand their nation "aim to make their citizens feel better and more confident about themselves by giving them a sense of belonging and a clear self-concept" (van Ham 2002: 253). The Trump Wall is branded according to modalities that are very similar to those used for location branding, which is not just advertising a nation's or a city's products, but is also about identity-formation, functioning pretty much in the same way as nation-building, in that it manages "identity, loyalty and image" (van Ham 2002: 255).

The Trump Wall has been circulating with the Trump label and, therefore, with all the aspects in terms of emotions and identity relating to Trump as a brand and a brand name, and as such it aims at resonating with the public. The whole Trump brand is constructed as a consumer brand but is also related to what Mazzarella calls Trump's tautological celebrity, or his "being famous for being famous" (Mazzarella 2019: 141), which is inextricably linked to the enjoyment that originates from "Trump" as a brand name. The "enjoyable visibility" of Trump's name also derives from the idea that Trump's brand name is singular, unique as well as self-referential, as it is personified by Trump himself, a meta-brand or "a brand about branding" (Dumenco 2017). Once he became president, Trump was well aware of the potential synergies between market and politics, and his name brand became one with the presidency:

> How do Trump brand values translate to the presidency? Simple: The brand that's about branding will just keeping throwing stuff to the wall to see if it sticks. Except the "stuff" now is politics. And policy. And national destiny.
>
> (Dumenco 2017)

Name-branding the Wall means bestowing on it the same aura of success, notoriety and privilege as Trump's own creations. If a "carefully created and chosen [brand] name can bring *inherent* and *immediate* value to the brand" (Kohli and LaBahn 1997: 67; emphasis in the original), then the Trump Wall is immediately linked to the pre-existing values attached to the name "Trump" and the objects it is famously associated with, for example, the Trump Tower. Like Trump's other brands, the Trump Wall comes to symbolise (or even, for many, *to be*) an object of privilege and enjoyment, like a luxury ("great" and "beautiful") home in Manhattan or a hotel. As a signifier, the name "Trump" conjures up feelings of enjoyment related to the brand, and Trump's public profile is inseparable from the idea itself of enjoyment. As noted by Mazzarella, the enjoyment implicit in the consumption of Trump's name-brand products derives from the merging of the enjoyment of the personal name of Trump the President and Trump as a name associated with a series of successful (and a few not-so-successful) products and services (2019: 113–117). The Trump Wall then becomes an object of enjoyment, even of visual enjoyment, for those who support it—indeed, for one Trump supporter, "The No.1 reason I voted for him was for the immigration… I want the wall. I want it to be seen in space, like the Chinese wall" (call to Laura Ingraham's radio show, Peters 2017). The Wall is therefore important not just because it prevents immigration, but because it needs to be *seen*.

Thus, through intertextual and interdiscursive chains and the ensuing discursive recontextualisation of certain recognisable cognitive structures, Trump manages to communicate the value and importance of his border to his audience. The audience is given a frame of reference which derives from the recontextualisation of a brand, the Trump brand, a process which is at the basis of the communication of corporate brands (Koller 2008), into the context of the wall. Crucially, in the light of the interdiscursive features of Trump's representations of his wall, the branding of the Trump Wall is not an ideologically moot or discursively isolated figment. Rather, the aesthetics of the wall contribute to the construction of the inclusive/exclusive nature of the nation. As a border dividing two nations and allegedly protecting the

USA, the Trump Wall is constructed in discourse to ostentatiously communicate the privilege of being American and of living on the "right" side of the wall. The border wall also excludes outsiders, and those who are allowed to cross it are given a privilege, that is, the right of entry to the USA. Trump's aesthetic is part of the axiological divide between us and them, the outsiders left out of the border, as the "beautiful" wall is an vainglorious display of the benefits reaped by the insiders and a proclamation of Trump's life as a winner (Vaillancourt 2017), a success story that he extends to all American citizens and one which the "losers" excluded from it cannot reach and can only glimpse at a distance—perhaps through the gaps between the wall's steel slats. Trump's aesthetic is powered by emotionality (Ratner 2020) and by the idea of success and its lavishness and boastful luxury, but it is an idea of beauty which is specifically his, and is demeaning of—and constructed in opposition to—other values, such as culture or science (Beres 2017).

Trump's branding of "his" wall and its (relative) success may be seen as evidence of the appeal that consumerism and marketing have for politics. While it may be claimed that all politics is now influenced by marketing and that marketing and advertising strategies are often used to "buy" consensus in the public sphere, in Trump's case consumerism and branding are used to exclude those who are considered non-Americans from the homeland. This may also be observed when the President visited again the border near San Diego, California on September 18, 2019, and on that occasion, Trump signed a section of the barrier (Figure 2.4).

In doing so, the wall becomes a celebrity item, with a rite, that of signing an autograph, typical of celebrity status and products: just as musicians sign their albums or writers sign their books, Trump is seen here as signing "his" wall and asserting his brand. Thus, the discursive construction of the Trump Wall can be explained by Dovi's notion of "name-brand populism." In American politics, where the electorate increasingly understands both social and political life in terms of consumerism and the marketplace, name-brand populism induces citizens to see their own citizenship as an exclusive privilege to defend and, conversely, a privilege that others should be denied. Dovi argues that this particular development of populism is based on three key features. The first is the "centrality of perception" (2018: 335), that is, what is important is the perceived value of the good, not necessarily its true value, which is one of the core tenets of name branding. It is this perception that evokes a certain emotional response in those who possess the good (and an opposite emotional reaction in those who do not). The second feature is the shared social identity induced by name brands, as name-brand populism unites those citizens who feel left out, marginalised and neglected by mainstream politics, or by the elite. The third feature is the reliance on "moment marketing," where an issue is created and then accompanied by

Figure 2.4 Former President Donald J. Trump signing a section of border fencing, Otay Mesa, San Diego, CA, September 18, 2019 (*Trump White House Archived*, Creative Commons).

sensationalism, violent language and a storm of messages on social media. At the basis of all this is the Trump Brand, a tripartite entity made up of "the boss, the independent and the luxurious" which has transmigrated from the world of real estate to that of TV and finally to politics. Following Dovi's argument, it can be said that the perceived quality of the wall, its appearance and all the fancy features associated with it as advertised by Trump outweigh whatever effectiveness as a barrier it might have.

The branding of the Trump Wall merges all of the functions that characterise borders: besides being a government infrastructure and a legal signpost for a nation's sovereignty, a border is also a geographical location and a powerful cultural symbol, and the Trump Wall becomes somehow a symbol of difference (for those outside it) and identification with certain values (for those inside it) which are not just values related to national identity, but to a certain social status conferred by belonging to the nation.

Notes

1 To put things in perspective, the same survey found that only 52% of Trump's supporters backed the deportation of illegal immigrants, while 48% said they

should be allowed to stay in the US legally. 48% of Trump's supporters asked for stronger law enforcement and better border security (Doherty 2016).

2 Coulter influenced Trump in some of his key proposals about immigration, something that she would proudly boast about and that Trump himself was ready to acknowledge (Beinart 2015; Hananoki 2015).

3 All of Trump's books have been co-authored with other writers, who no doubt did most or all of the writing. In the specific case of *The Art of the Deal*, its actual authorship is still disputed, with both Schwartz and its publisher, Random House, claiming that Trump wrote no part of it. However, given that Schwartz followed Trump closely and was personally involved with him for eighteen months while working on the book (Mayer 2016), there is little doubt that what was written in the book, as in all other books by Trump, reflected Trump's own language and ideology quite closely.

4 The expansion of the Trump brand and of various other brands associated with him continued unabated during Trump's presidency, as the growing number of trademarks registered worldwide by Trump's firms attests (Hakim and Lee 2017).

3 The progressive rhetoric of borders

While Trump's border rhetoric aimed at demonising migrants and advocating an ethnocentric view of the nation, it could be expected that Democrats, and progressives in general, would espouse a diametrically opposed border policy, or at least one not based on aggressive nationalism and nativism. It is certainly true that Democrats have traditionally been accused by Trump and the Republicans of being "soft" on immigration and crime and of supporting "open borders," two issues which were always connected in conservative discourses. Ultimately, however, the picture was not so straightforward, at least as far as the mainstream Democratic culture is concerned, and key Democratic figures supported border policies which were much less inclusive than might have been hoped.

This chapter addresses the representation of borders as a discourse topic by mainstream Democrats and progressives, and how this representation projects an idea of the nation which, as will be shown, is only partly alternative to Trump's. It will do so by analysing a dataset of the most important statements on borders by three key progressive politicians: Bernie Sanders, the independent Senator from Vermont and two-time candidate for the Democratic presidential nomination; Hillary Clinton, the Democratic 2016 presidential candidate who was defeated by Donald Trump; and Joe Biden, elected as the 46th President of the USA in 2020. While the three politicians do differ in some important issues (in particular, Sanders' own brand of "Democratic Socialism" places him at odds with the more centrist platforms of both Clinton and Biden), their position on borders may be seen on the whole to exemplify the mainstream liberal or progressive stance—and as such has been lambasted by Trump and the Republicans as supporting "open borders," neglectful of the real needs of the American people, and oblivious to the dangers posed to the nation by immigrants and other people crossing the border. In their turn, before and during Trump's mandate, Democrats attacked the former President's border and immigration policies, including wall building, along two main arguments: (1) the

DOI: 10.4324/9781003287971-4

wall was ineffective in stopping migration and was a waste of money, and (2) some measures taken at the borders, first of all family separation, were utterly inhumane and ran against the values of the USA as a nation of immigrants. Democrats countered the Trump Wall with an idea of borders based on modernity and technology (or a "smart border"), using images of children or whole families in cages because of Trump's border policy to whip up indignation among large segments of the US electorate.

Democrats and "open borders"

The modern rhetoric of "open borders" is in many respects an offshoot of globalisation. Neoliberal economics supported the free flow of capital and labour and any barrier to it, including borders, was considered to be an obstacle to be removed. Open borders have thus long been the flagship issue of free market groups on the right, which "have advocated for liberalizing migration on the grounds of market rationality and economic freedom" (Nagle 2018). At the same time, open borders have also been supported on the basis of basic human rights, such as the right to move freely (Jones 2019). Freedom of movement between nations would allow immigrants to escape misery and move to richer nations, and opposition to the wall or other measures favouring border restrictions in the USA was exemplified by the slogan "no human is illegal." Right-wing and populist narratives brand the rhetoric of open borders as a trademark of progressives. According to these narratives, open borders would allow unlimited numbers of migrants to enter, thus supposedly putting US citizens' livelihood and security at risk and threatening to make the nation impure and chaotic—ethnically, socially, culturally and linguistically. Trump himself often criticised Democrats for their border policies in connection with immigration, claiming that they supported "open borders." During the 2016 Presidential campaign, Trump claimed that Clinton was in favour of "totally open borders," which have caused or would cause a rise in criminality and "will destroy jobs and drive down wages for everyone" (Speech: Donald Trump in New York, NY, June 22, 2016). Clinton herself had provided Trump with ample ammunition regarding her alleged support for open borders. In a speech she gave to a Brazilian bank in 2013 and revealed by WikiLeaks in October 2016, she argued that

> My dream is a hemispheric common market, with open trade and open borders, some time in the future with energy that is as green and sustainable as we can get it, powering growth and opportunity for every person in the hemisphere.

(WikiLeaks 2016)

While Clinton was indexing the neoliberal ethos of free trade rather than allowing immigration, this statement made it very easy for Trump to associate Clinton and the Democrats with open borders and to accuse them of opening the floodgates to illegal immigration. Once he became president, Trump's rhetoric did not change. In praising House Republicans who opposed the Democrats' attempt to override his veto of Congress' resolution to terminate the declaration of emergency on the southern border, Trump tweeted in March 2019:

> Thank you to the House Republicans for sticking together and the BIG WIN today on the Border. Today's vote simply reaffirms Congressional Democrats are the party of Open Borders, Drugs and Crime!
> (@realDonaldTrump, March 26, 2019)

This statement is part of Trump's rhetoric of fear, in which he, as discussed in Chapter 2, associates unsafe borders with immigration, crime and terrorism. Indeed, the open borders moniker could be used very effectively in the Republican narrative when attacking Democrats as a party favouring immigration, crime and low wages for US workers. In turn, Democrats were at pains to fend off Trump's accusations of being soft on border security and, whether by conviction or convenience, opposed the whole notion of open borders. In fact, Democrats have often advocated strong border policies limiting immigrants' access to the USA and have repeatedly passed or supported legislation to that effect (Sherman 2016; Qiu 2018). In a famous July 2015 interview with Vox's director Ezra Klein, Bernie Sanders explicitly argued the case against open borders by linking the notion to capitalism:

> Open borders? No, that's a Koch brothers proposal (…) It would make everybody in America poorer—you're doing away with the concept of a nation state, and I don't think there's any country in the world that believes in that. If you believe in a nation state or in a country called the United States or UK or Denmark or any other country, you have an obligation in my view to do everything we can to help poor people. What right-wing people in this country would love is an open-border policy. Bring in all kinds of people, work for $2 or $3 an hour, that would be great for them. I don't believe in that. I think we have to raise wages in this country, I think we have to do everything we can to create millions of jobs.
>
> (Klein 2015)

Sanders' argument against open borders is not very different from Trump's on three levels: (1) Sanders' mention of the Koch brothers[1] points to the typically populist anti-establishment rhetoric; (2) through open borders, the influx of millions of immigrants would drive down wages for US workers; (3) without borders, there is no nation, as "you're doing away with the concept of a nation state, and I don't think there's any country in the world that believes in that." Sanders would again oppose open borders on economic grounds in 2019, when he declared:

> Oh my god, there's a lot of poverty in this world, and you're going to have people from all over the world. And I don't think that's something that we can do at this point. Can't do it.
>
> (Lemon 2019)

Though Clinton also highlighted the relationship between borders and nation and opposed open borders herself, she moved away from Trump's perceived harsh rhetoric by emphasising the need to show humanity and fairness towards immigrants while at the same time upholding a system based on laws:

> Look, I know very personally how hard this issue is, how deep the emotions run. I'm not talking about open borders, I'm talking about immigration laws enforced with fairness and respect for human rights. Of course, security and the rule of law must be upheld. Of course, nations have a right and duty to control their borders, in concert with their neighbors. But we can't let fear or bias force us to give up the values that have made our democracies both great and good.
>
> (Clinton 2018)

While supporting humane treatment of migrants, Clinton denies any kind of legitimacy to open borders as a concept. In arguing that "nations have a right and duty to control their borders," she aligns herself with the classic concept of borders as an essential part of the nation. Clinton rejects open borders, supporting a reformed and fair immigration system:

> On both sides of the Atlantic, we need reform. Not open borders, but immigration laws enforced with fairness and respect for human rights. We can't let fear or bias force us to give up the values that have made our democracies both great and good.
>
> (@HillaryClinton, November 23, 2018)

The big difference between Clinton and Trump is of course the wildly different emphasis on human rights as a matter of humanity and law. Open borders are construed by the Democratic leadership as opposed to what a nation as an institution, with all its laws and practices, is all about.

Backtracking on the notion of borders through "open borders" would thus mean reneging on the very idea of a nation. However, the brutal implications of a closed border are somehow mitigated by upholding the "rule of law" as well as humanity and respect for the human rights of those who claim immigrant status.

From nation separation to family separation. Borders and the strength of the "nation of immigrants"

Between April and June 2018, the Trump administration enforced the so-called family separation policy, whereby families with children who were arrested while crossing the border between Mexico and the USA illegally would have their child or children taken from them and held in separate detention centres. This policy was enforced as part of the "zero tolerance" approach that the Trump administration intended to adopt towards illegal immigration and the crimes allegedly related to it, and it was meant to serve as a deterrence to those who intended to cross the border. The policy was immediately controversial, attracting harsh criticism from many quarters: children were taken away from their families when they were caught crossing the borders and could not be reunited with them for months, while their whereabouts were often not known. Photos of crying immigrant children being torn from their parents or penned in steel cages struck a chord with the public. In June 2020, Trump finally relented, signing an executive order reuniting families (Davis and Shear 2019: 252–279), but not before opinion polls showed that a huge majority of the US public disagreed with Trump's policy (Sides 2018).

The controversy surrounding Trump's family separation policy provided the Democrats with some effective political and rhetorical firepower. Even after Trump withdrew his family separation policy, Clinton attacked him fiercely, becoming an advocate of the rights of children separated from their families. She did so by employing highly emotional language which highlighted the inhumanity of Trump's policies: associating borders with the pain suffered by these children, she spoke of the "unspeakable cruelty inflicted on undocumented families arriving at our southern border, including separating children, some as young as eight months, from their parents" (Clinton 2018). In a series of tweets between June and November 2018, she reiterated Trump's inhumanity at the border several times. In the Democratic rhetoric, the border becomes the symbol of Trump's unjust cruelty towards fellow human beings:

> This #GivingTuesday, consider giving to support organizations that have spent the last few months working tirelessly to reunite families the

administration has separated at the border. Over 200 children are still waiting to be reunited with loved ones.

(@HillaryClinton, November 27, 2018)

Trump has made it worse with cruel abuses at the border, detaining children and separating them from their families. It's one of the most shameful moments in our history.

(@HillaryClinton, November 23, 2018)

By describing family separation, Clinton wants to communicate emotions of sadness (for the children) and rage against those who subjected them to such suffering): family separation at the borders is "one of the most shameful moments in our history," a humanitarian crisis." And "devastating to even imagine." Clinton attacks Trump's border policy on family separation by emphasising certain universal feelings of love and affection:

I am horrified and heartbroken by what is happening to immigrant kids and families because of this administration's disastrous policies.

(@HillaryClinton, June 1, 2018)

We should be heartbroken to see families torn apart, but we should not be hopeless.

(@HillaryClinton, June 18, 2018)

Every parent who has ever held a child in their arms, every human being with a sense of compassion and decency, should be outraged.

(@HillaryClinton, June 18, 2018)

Fighting against inhumane conditions at the border is a matter of conscience and law.

(@HillaryClinton, July 4, 2019)

Clinton's emotional plea for the children separated from their families is legitimised by highlighting a certain notion of the USA as a welcoming and compassionate nation. This idea of the nation, constructed as alternative to Trump's, is foregrounded in discourse by creating a collective identity through the use of an "inclusive we," that is, the first plural person pronoun which includes her audience (meaning all US citizens) and herself, who share a similar concern for the plight of children:

I still believe in the vision we share for our country. We will elect politicians and enact legislation to protect the most vulnerable among us—but first, we have to address the urgent needs of families at the center of this crisis.

(@HillaryClinton, June 18, 2018)

There is no more important test of our country than the way we treat the most vulnerable among us, especially children.

(@HillaryClinton, June 1, 2018)

We should be a better country than one that tears families apart, turns a blind eye to women fleeing domestic violence, and treats frightened children as a means to a political end.

(@HillaryClinton, June 18, 2018)

The test of any nation is how we treat the most vulnerable among us.

(@HillaryClinton, June 18, 2018)

The discourse strategy of mentioning children aims at raising feelings of humanity among the electorate. Joe Biden uses a very similar rhetoric of compassion in his discourse. The photo of a woman pleading as her husband and daughter are swept away by the Rio Grande while trying to cross the border between Mexico and Texas prompted Biden to express his disgust in a tweet:

This image is gut-wrenching. The cruelty we're seeing at our border is unconscionable. History will judge how we respond to the Trump Administration's treatment of immigrant families & children—we can't be silent. This isn't who we are. This is not America.

(@JoeBiden, June 26, 2019)

Biden again mentioned "families & children," drawing attention to the cruel events taking place at the border because of Trump's policies. His newly elected administration showed a similar concern with the pleas of families when the first measures regarding borders and immigration were announced. When Biden sent his Immigration Bill to Congress, the official "Fact Sheet" posted January 20, 2021 on the White House website and entitled "President Biden Sends Immigration Bill to Congress as Part of His Commitment to Modernize our Immigration System," included measures to "Keep families together" and intended to reform "the family-based immigration system," eliminating "the so-called '3 and 10-year bars,' and other provisions that keep families apart" (White House 2021b). The bill also reinstated "the Central American Minors program to reunite children with U.S. relatives and creates a Central American Family Reunification

Parole Program to more quickly unite families with approved family sponsorship petitions" (White House 2021b).

The difference between Trump and Democrats regarding borders is also one between how emotions are played out in language. As seen in Chapter 2, Trump's discourse is largely based on anger and, often, hatred directed towards migrants. On the other hand, lexical choices based on pity and compassion towards immigrants take centre stage when Democrats attack Trump's immigration and border policy: Clinton herself is "horrified and heartbroken" as family separation is "devastating," "shameful" and "unspeakable cruelty." Democrats stressed the need to treat migrants humanely, highlighting the cries of children forcibly separated from their parents. They aim at delegitimising Trump's discourse by using highly emotional verbal (and often visual) images of children and families torn apart at the border.

The basis of Clinton's and Biden's continued attention to "family separation" of immigrant families lies in the Democrats' own version of what has been considered one of the founding American values: family. Family values have been a constant presence in political life in the USA for at least the last 40 years or so: they are a powerful rhetorical tool and an ideological rallying cry of the Republican leadership and have often taken centre stage in the political battleground between Democrats and Republicans (May 2003). Former Presidents Ronald Reagan and George W. Bush constantly presented themselves as defenders of family values, and with them the nuclear family was celebrated (as well as promoted financially through specific welfare measures) as the true social asset of the nation with surefire appeal for voters. Even former Democratic President Bill Clinton, who campaigned for "non-traditional" families, ended up supporting traditional family values (Stacey 1996: 3–4, 54–56). The Democrats' recontextualisation of family values takes place against a political backdrop in which Trump made family separation the core of his border and immigration policies. Thus, by showing their sympathy to the plight of children and their families, Democrats intended to highlight the supposed inhumanity of a president who, as they implied, did not care about a truly American value. In this sense, Clinton, Biden and Sanders were seemingly filling the values vacuum left by Trump. Trump's later half-hearted condemnation of family separation in June 2018 signalled a shift in priorities in the Republican agenda: while Evangelical and Methodist leaders condemned the President's ruthless policy, Trump prioritised his zero-tolerance policy on migrants and demoted "family values," and a majority of Republicans agreed with him (Talbot 2018; Wagner 2018).

However, there is a key difference between the typical Republican pro-family stance and the Democrats' discourse during the family separation crisis: while the family values supported by Republicans traditionally referred to American families, the families defended by Democrats were not American, but immigrants from outside the USA. At the same time, the Democrats' defence of immigrant families' rights on humanitarian grounds is often linked to the notion that the USA is a nation of immigrants, implicitly foregrounding the ethnic variety of the American nation and turning it into an asset (an electoral asset too, given the traditional preference of most minorities living in the USA for Democrats). Biden himself focussed on this concept several times, praising immigration in the USA on his official Twitter page (@JoeBiden) as essential to the strength of the American nation:

> Immigration has always made us stronger—it's essential to who we are. But Donald Trump has waged an assault on our values as a nation of immigrants. As president, I'll undo Trump's damage and put our values back at the heart of our immigration system.
>
> (@JoeBiden, December 11, 2019)

> Donald Trump's inhumane, fear-based immigration policies are a stain on our nation. We have to get him out of the White House and ensure our laws reflect our values as a nation of immigrants.
>
> (@JoeBiden, February 16, 2020)

> Immigrants have always made our country stronger. Our diversity is, and has always been, our greatest strength. Donald Trump doesn't get that—we need a president who does.
>
> (@JoeBiden, June 24, 2020)

> America is a nation that values immigrants. It is and has always been one of our greatest strengths. We need a president who understands that.
>
> (@JoeBiden, October 20, 2020)

Biden stressed the need for certain measures in favour of immigrants already in the USA on the basis of the roots and heritage of the American nation. By contrast, the concept of America's strength as based on its immigrant population is something that can rarely (if ever) be found in Trump's rhetoric. Biden turns the frequent association of the presence of immigrants with the country's strength into one of the founding values of the USA as a nation ("But Donald Trump has waged an assault on *our values* as a nation of immigrants. As president, I'll undo Trump's damage and put *our values* back at the heart of our immigration system"; "We have to get [Trump] out of the White House and ensure our laws reflect *our values as a nation of immigrants*"). Thus, Biden's emphasis on diversity and immigration as a value places his discourse in a moral framework and puts him on the moral high ground for attacking Trump.

The moral basis of Biden's and the Democrats' attack on Trump about family separation appeals to the large minorities in the USA who descended from immigrants or had recently become American citizens. However, the Democrats' support for "the most vulnerable" individuals, that is children separated from their families, derives from what Lakoff calls the "Nurturant Parent" model of family life. According to Lakoff, American society is dominated by and conceptualises itself in two family-based moral systems, Strict Father Morality and Nurturant Parent Morality (Lakoff 2002). Both models give priority to certain metaphors to express certain values, and these metaphors are the basis of different moral systems. Strict Father Morality assumes that the world is a dangerous and highly competitive place, and in order to survive and succeed there must be strict moral rules and a system of rewards and punishments for those who respectively follow and violate these rules. This system expresses itself in discourse through a series of metaphorical scenarios (e.g. Moral Strength, Moral Authority, Moral Order, Moral Boundaries), and these metaphors map out in discourse the social structure and the behaviour that citizens are expected to follow. On the other hand, Nurturant Parent Morality is based on a model of parental care for children. Providing care and protection from dangers and evils are a key aspect of being a parent. In this model, children do not learn primarily through rewards and punishment, but through sympathy and protection. The model crucially develops a moral attitude to the world, and people should develop certain conditions to make the world a hospitable place through nurturance, empathy, compassion and fair distribution—all qualities that result in metaphorical scenarios which are diametrically opposite to those arising from Strict Father Morality. Lakoff argues that these two moral systems are projected onto politics by the Nation as Family metaphor, whereby the authority that a nation projects onto its citizens is metaphorised into a family metaphor, which sees the Government as a Parent and the Citizens as its Children (Lakoff 2002: 154–161). The two moral systems, the Strict Father and the Nurturant Parent, share this metaphorical projection of the nation but they do so in obviously different ways and according to the differences in their moral attitude.

The Democratic leaders construct the nation as a family and the nation's leaders as nurturant parents who have certain values and moral obligations to look after their vulnerable children, while bad leaders do not fulfil these values and obligations ("Trump has made it worse with cruel abuses at the border, detaining children and separating them from their families"). While migrant children crossing the border are not

American (or not American yet), the sense of nurturing and compassion is raised by Democrats and spread to the newcomers through the repeated claim that the USA is a "nation of immigrants." This aims at communicating a sense of moral duty towards the children separated from their families at the border, and those who promote the family separation policy are accordingly condemned as inhuman and lacking compassion. Thus, while the "Nation as Family" metaphor may seem to be only partly relevant to the Democrats' discourse (migrant children are not the nation's children), Democratic leaders still project a sense of the nation as a nurturant parent expressing feelings or compassion, for example, when Clinton argues that "We should be a better country than one that tears families apart, turns a blind eye to women fleeing domestic violence, and treats frightened children as a means to a political end" or that "There is no more important test of our country than the way we treat the most vulnerable among us, especially children."

In highlighting the pleas and suffering of children separated from their families, Democrats use one of the typical conservative strategies as outlined by Republican strategist Frank Luntz to create effective messages for the electorate, that is, mentioning children in political discourse. In his book, Luntz argues that voters interpret messages on the basis of the interaction between the emotions occurring at the time and the values that voters have acquired as part of their family experiences. One of Luntz's key rules for successful communication is summarised in his dictum "It's about the children," as he firmly believed that the electorate, especially women, would be more prone to listen to messages mentioning children, even when the message itself has nothing to do with children:

> To women, children are the face of the future and the embodiment of tomorrow. From a balanced budget to welfare reform, child-centered arguments consistently score better with women than economic or more factually based messaging. This applies not only to education, health care, and the environment, but also to "hard" issues such as taxes and foreign policy.
>
> (Luntz 2007: 44)

Borders and border security are certainly one such "hard" issue, an issue that also ties in with family values because it is borders that caused the separation of children from their families. Thus, introducing the family separation policy in the context of border security became the perfect scenario for the Democrats to attack Trump on his own turf: Democrats foregrounded family values and emotions related to children in discourse by attacking the cruelty of Trump's border policy.

The modern (and effective) border

The Democrats' attack on Trump's family separation policy and their defence of immigrants on humanitarian grounds were often accompanied in their border and immigration discourse by the need to protect the nation and provide it with security. The Democrats' rhetoric often aims at striking a balance between the two discourses, that of family values and that of national security.

This balance could be seen in Clinton's own presidential agenda in 2016. In outlining the need to reform the immigration system in the face of a huge visa backlog and to reunite families who were split by the borders, Clinton supports

> comprehensive reform [which] will keep our communities safer. It will give law enforcement the resources they need to strengthen our borders, focus on crime and criminals, and harness technology to address threats to our national security.
>
> (Clinton and Kaine 2016: 186)

Clinton's discussion focussing on the discourse of borders includes the issue of safety, security and crime, as if these were a natural occurrence at the borders, which need to be strengthened (implying that they are weak now) as they are vital to "our national security."

Sanders developed a similar approach to borders, immigration and security. As argued earlier, Sanders did not really support the notion of open borders, which he believed threatened the wages of US workers and undermined the very idea of the nation. When he talked about border policy, however, inclusion and security merge in discourse. One of the "Key Issues" of Sanders' official campaign website for the 2020 Democratic primaries, berniesanders.com, called "A Welcoming and Safe America for All," is a good example of the attempt to balance these two discourses, where the USA is, in fact, both "welcoming" (immigrants) and "safe" (for US nationals): "welcoming" evokes emotions of affection and compassion, while supporting a "safe" America recalls the discourse of security at the borders. Starting with the statement that "This country is a nation of immigrants," the document proposes that Trump's policies be dismantled, as they both criminalise and terrorise immigrants:

> Stop all construction of the racist and ineffective wall on the U.S.-Mexico Border and instead rely on cost-effective and innovative methods to counter the real threats of drug importation and human trafficking, not manufactured ones targeting the most vulnerable.
>
> (Sanders 2020)

Sanders views the current situation at the USA–Mexico border in terms of "humanitarian crisis" and "border militarization." By contrast, he proposes to address the issue of border crossings "as a civil matter," arguing that "We will exercise due process at the border and establish a humane and fair review process for asylum claims." Furthermore, the emphasis on "cost-effective and innovative methods" at the border points to an ethics of efficiency and modernity which, as will be discussed later, contributes to constructing a discourse on border security alternative to, but not necessarily less stringent than, Trump's expensive plans.

The balance between being "welcoming" and ensuing safety is made even more evident by the visual representation of Sanders during one of his visits to the USA–Mexico border during the 2016 Democratic primaries. In the photos and videos of the event in Nogales, Arizona, circulating in the press and online, the candidate for the Democratic nomination speaks with the border in the background and is joined by a politician, US Rep. Raúl Grijalva, and by Santa Cruz County Sheriff Tony Estrada. On the surface, Sanders' image is no different from that projected by Trump's own visit to the border, as discussed in Chapter 2. However, while Trump is accompanied by a white male officer, Sanders is with two members of the Latino community, and their presence communicates ethnic inclusiveness and mitigates the sense of law and order usually connected with the border.

Figure 3.1 Bernie Sanders speaking near the border in Nogales, Arizona, March 19, 2016 (Associated Press).

The opposition to Trump's wall and the need for more humane immigration reform also featured in Joe Biden's presidential campaign. As testified by two tweets, Biden opposed Trump's wall on the basis of its inefficiency:

> We must secure our borders, but "build the wall" is a slogan divorced from reality. We need to focus on improving screening procedures at our legal ports of entry & making smart investments in border technology. These policies will do more for our security than a wall ever could.
>
> (@JoeBiden, June 25, 2019)

> A border wall is the physical embodiment of @realDonaldTrump's inability to develop effective immigration policy. His use of Department of Defense funds for the wall is a phony answer to the real challenges we face—and he knows it.
>
> (@JoeBiden, July 27, 2019)

While Trump's wall is "divorced from reality," Biden advocates "smart investments in border technology" and "effective immigration policy," thus implicitly acknowledging the dangers of a lax immigration and border policy. In attacking Trump's plan, Biden reiterates that "We must secure our borders" and "These policies will do more for our security than a wall ever could," again stressing the priority given to security when addressing borders, while immigrants themselves are expected to follow a lawful path to access the USA ("our *legal* ports of entry"). Thus, Trump's wall is not attacked just because it is inhumane, but also because it is not effective. Through his repeated use of the "inclusive we" ("*We* must secure *our* borders … *we* need to focus … *our* legal ports of entry …" "the real challenges *we* face"), Biden also emphasises the collective endeavour and concerns of both his government and US citizens as he employs the "syntax of hegemony," identified by Billig and discussed in Chapter 1 earlier, which is a typical trait of nationalism and of the consensus that politicians communicate and try to achieve in their discourse.

Biden's emphasis on border security has merged with humanitarian concerns since his first days in office. On January 20, 2021 he pledged to reverse some of Trump's policies on immigration, including the so-called Muslim ban, which prevented the arrival of citizens from some Muslim-majority countries, and to preserve the Deferred Action for Childhood Arrivals (DACA) program, which allowed undocumented migrants who came to the USA as children to live, work and study legally (De Witte 2021).[2] In a "Proclamation" posted on the White House webpage on January 20, 2021, Biden declared the "Termination Of Emergency With

Respect To The Southern Border Of The United States" (White House 2021a), deciding to end funding for border wall construction. Both in the "Proclamation" and the "Fact Sheet" relating to it (White House 2021b), the new administration focused on border reform by stressing its intention to protect immigrants already working in the USA, end family separation, prosecute criminal organisations, and fast-track and review applications for US citizenship. While the prosecution of cross-border criminal organisations echoed Trump's emphasis on the immigration-crime nexus, the lexis and the tone used by the Biden administration was very different from that used by Trump in his border policy. In the first two paragraphs of a "Fact Sheet" posted on the White House webpage on January 20, 2021, Biden highlighted the need to introduce innovative practices at the border:

> The U.S. Citizenship Act of 2021 establishes a new system to responsibly manage and secure our border, keep our families and communities safe, and better manage migration across the Hemisphere.
>
> President Biden is sending a bill to Congress on day one to restore humanity and American values to our immigration system. The bill provides hardworking people who enrich our communities every day and who have lived here for years, in some cases for decades, an opportunity to earn citizenship. The legislation modernizes our immigration system, and prioritizes keeping families together, growing our economy, responsibly managing the border with smart investments, addressing the root causes of migration from Central America, and ensuring that the United States remains a refuge for those fleeing persecution. The bill will stimulate our economy while ensuring that every worker is protected. The bill creates an earned path to citizenship for our immigrant neighbors, colleagues, parishioners, community leaders, friends, and loved ones—including Dreamers and the essential workers who have risked their lives to serve and protect American communities.
>
> (White House 2021b)

Biden distances himself from the policies of the previous administration through two implicatures: (1) by "sending a bill to Congress on day one to *restore humanity and American values* to our immigration system," he suggested that Trump's immigration system was inhumane and un-American. In fact, by prioritising keeping families together, Biden emphasises the importance of the values attached to the notion of "family," something that Trump himself was constantly attacked for, as discussed earlier; (2) Biden also expressed his intention to "*modernize* our immigration system," implying that the current system was obsolete and ineffective, and needed to be renewed. There is a reiteration of the idea that borders should be efficient and properly managed: border management is mentioned three times in the two opening paragraphs of the "Fact Sheet" ("a new system to responsibly *manage* and secure our border, keep our families and communities safe, and better *manage* migration across the Hemisphere," "responsibly *managing* the border with smart investments"). The verb "manage" is used twice again in the same text ("It authorizes the DHS Secretary to develop and implement *a strategy to manage and secure* the southern border between ports of entry"; "*Manage the border* and protect border communities"). In these two last examples, the concept of a properly working and managed border is explicitly related to the notion of security, safety and protection along the borders and inside the USA.

A "well-managed border" was also at the centre of the two "Fact Sheets" posted on the White House webpage on July 27 and 29, 2021, called respectively "The Biden Administration Blueprint for a Fair, Orderly and Humane Immigration System" and "The Collaborative Migration Management Strategy." The former document opens by stating that "The United States can have an orderly, secure, and well-managed border while treating people fairly and humanely" (White House 2021c). The phrasing seems to give the same emphasis to the effectiveness and safety of borders and to fair treatment of migrants, but the latter is slightly backgrounded as it is placed in a subordinate clause at the end of the sentence. The intention is that of "ENSURING A SECURE, HUMANE AND WELL-MANAGED BORDER" as "The United States can allow people to exercise their legal right to apply for asylum while also reducing irregular migration and maintaining an orderly, secure, and well-managed border." Biden also intends to invest more money in "smarter border security measures, like border technology and modernization of land ports of entry, that are proven to be more effective at improving safety and security at the border." The latter document, "The Collaborative Migration Management Strategy," is described as "the first U.S. government strategy focused on strengthening cooperative efforts to manage safe, orderly, and humane migration in North and Central America" (White House 2021d). The avowed intentions also include "investing in migration management" and "Foster[ing] secure and humane management of borders." Again, humanitarian discourse and safety discourse are merged ("safe, orderly, and humane migration"). What emerges quite clearly from the documents published by the White House is that the Biden Administration projected an idea of modernity in the US borders (borders, of course, mainly mean the USA–Mexico border). The language in which Biden speaks of borders and on how immigration should be addressed in their context is characterised by a constant preoccupation with efficiency and efficacy. In fact, in the "Fact Sheet" discussed earlier, Biden speaks of "modernizing" the border through technology:

PRIORITIZE SMART BORDER CONTROLS

Supplement existing border resources with technology and infrastructure. The legislation builds on record budget allocations for immigration enforcement by authorizing additional funding for the Secretary of DHS to develop and implement a plan to deploy technology to expedite screening and enhance the ability to identify narcotics and other contraband at every land, air, and sea port of entry. (…) The bill expands family case management programs, reduces immigration court backlogs, expands training for immigration judges, and improves technology for immigration courts.

(White House 2021b)

In all these "Fact Sheets" Trump's concept of a border wall is replaced by a *modern* border, where technology and infrastructure can handle the human flows in and out of the nation (as well as stemming the activities of criminal organisations) in an orderly fashion through what would become a "smart border."

With Democrats' leadership, the effective management of security at the borders become the key recontextualised discourse when talking about the borders in the context of the discourse of the nation. Thus, borders become the point of convergence of discourses of management, efficiency and security. Biden's constant emphasis on managing borders through overwording and repetition also denotes a degree of anxiety about border control, implying that, on the one hand, borders can be a source of danger, and on the other hand, that the new administration stresses its power and prerogative to control the nation's borders and regulate immigration in general. The discourse in which Biden constructs this is still one which prioritises the nation and its territorial and institutional integrity:

We will always be a nation of borders, and we will enforce our immigration laws in a way that is fair and just. We will continue to work to fortify an orderly immigration system.

(White House 2021c)

Biden's emphasis on the modernisation and management of borders seems to be a direct answer to the worries about immigration and open borders which years of right-wing propaganda had fuelled in large sectors of the American electorate. However, there is more to it. By using words such as "manage," "modernisation," "smart" and "technology" so frequently, the Biden administration was highlighting concepts which are quite typical of the neoliberal vocabulary. The frequent use of these words indicates the recontextualisation of a certain discourse when talking about borders: borders become imbued with concepts which are commonly applied to a discourse of neoliberal modernity and to efficient markets and economies.

Notes

1 Charles and David Koch (the latter died in 2019) amassed one of the largest fortunes in the USA and have been very active in funding conservative causes and think-tanks since the 1980s.
2 Trump had tried to shut down the DACA program altogether on September 5, 2017, but a ruling of the Supreme Court reinstated it fully.

Conclusions

In their representation of borders as part of the discourse of the nation, Trump and the Democrats display different ideas of how the border should work, especially in relation to welcoming (or not welcoming) foreigners to the USA. What Trump's and the Democrats' discourses on borders share is their common concern about security. This notion emerges following different modalities and recontextualisations in the two sets of discourses.

Through the Trump Wall, the border, a key structure of the nation in geopolitical terms, becomes a commodity: the Trump Wall is built to keep "illegal immigrants" and other supposedly dangerous individuals out of the USA, and this will bring financial benefits and lower crime rates. However, the "beautiful" Trump Wall is also an object judged by its aesthetic value: by aligning the institutional discourse with that of the Trump brand, the former US president presents the border wall, allegedly one of the nation's most important infrastructures, as if it were his own creature, one of the artefacts bearing his name. In many respects,

> Trump stands for the merger of private capital and state sovereignty, so that the State should ultimately become part of the Trump brand— American democracy is the new Trump Steaks, grilled to a crisp at Mar-a-Lago—and a worldwide platform for his ongoing reality show.
>
> (Schuster 2017)

The Trump Wall suggests the exclusivity associated with those who are protected by it, just like the customers of a Trump hotel or resort: US citizens.

Democratic leaders, on the other hand, support the notion of a "smart" and "modern" border, one where access is regulated in an orderly manner and in the name of a neoliberal ethos based on efficiency and cost-effectiveness. Sanders, Clinton and Biden insist on the need to protect the USA at the borders with the help of technology, not walls. Applications to

DOI: 10.4324/9781003287971-5

enter the USA would also be processed in an orderly manner, taking care of children and families, in direct opposition to Trump's family separation policy, all the while emphasising the former president's inhumane handling of border issues. The Democrats' discourse on borders had a strong moral basis, one founded on true American values in which humanity and compassion for the pleas of immigrant children and families are foregrounded; this notion was constructed in the context of a proposed border policy based on better and cost-effective border management, which would make the border "modern" and "smart," entirely unlike Trump's ineffective and inhumane wall.

While Democrats constantly opposed the Trump Wall before and during Trump's mandate, their leadership shared with the former president a common concern with border security. The articulation of borders as a topic in the discourse of the nation by both Trump and the Democrats shows that mainstream political leaders in the USA continually engage with the representation of threats to the public and to social order and, for this reason, contribute (and *respond*) to the construction of collective insecurity (Béland 2007). A common idea of what a nation should be and the role of borders in it underlies this shared discourse: it is through borders that sovereignty of a nation is established and renewed on its territory, and it is through borders that a nation's rule of law should never falter, because borders legitimise the very existence of the nation. This renewed idea of the nation's sovereignty seems to be closely connected to a process of "othering," or the alienisation of the foreign, non-US subject: security implies a danger coming from people outside the nation, and borders are inevitably and constantly represented as a potential source of this danger. In the Trump era and its immediate aftermath, border security has become a stable feature of US mainstream political discourse, and any mainstream discourse of the nation seems to be appealing to it continually.

References

Agnew, John. 2008. "Borders on the Mind: Re-framing Border Thinking." *Ethics & Global Politics* 1(4): 175–191. doi: 10.3402/egp.v1i4.1892

AMA (American Marketing Association). 2020. "Definitions of Marketing." www. ama.org/the-definition-of-marketing-what-is-marketing/#:~:text=Definit ion%20of%20Brand,from%20those%20of%20other%20sellers

Anderson, Benedict. 1991. *Imagined Communities*, rev. ed. London: Verso.

Anderson, James, and Liam O'Dowd. 1999. "Borders, Border Regions and Territoriality: Contradictory Meanings and Changing Significance." *Regional Studies* 33(7): 593–604.

Anderson, Malcolm. 1996. *Frontiers: Territory and State Formation in the Modern World.* Oxford: Polity Press.

Beinart, Peter. 2015. "It's Not Just Trump." *The Atlantic*, December 9, 2015. www. theatlantic.com/politics/archive/2015/12/before-donald-trump-therewas-ann-coulter/419517/

Béland, Daniel. 2007. "Insecurity and Politics: A Framework." *Canadian Journal of Sociology/Cahiers canadiens de sociologie* 32(3): 317–340.

Beres, Louise René. 2017. "Aesthetics and Politics: Donald Trump's Idea of Art and Beauty." *OUP Blog*, September 16, 2017. https://blog.oup.com/2017/09/aesthetics-politics-donald-trump-beauty/

Besanvalle, James. 2020. "13 Disturbing Things Trump Has Described as 'Beautiful' that Aren't Beautiful at All." *Indy100*, July 23, 2020. www.indy100.com/news/donald-trump-beautiful-9634036

Bevan, Tom. 2016. "Donald Trump's First TV Ad: I Will "Cut The Head Off" ISIS And Take The Oil." *RealClearPolitics*, January 4, 2016. www.realclearpolit ics.com/video/2016/01/04/donald_trumps_first_tv_ad_of_the_2016_campa ign.html

Billig, Michael. 1995. *Banal Nationalism*. London: Sage.

Brown, Wendy. 2010. *Walled States, Waning Sovereignty*. New York: Zone Books.

Castells, Manuel. 1989. *The Informational City: Information Technology, Economic Restructuring, and the Urban-regional Process.* Oxford: Blackwell.

Charteris-Black, Jonathan. 2006. "Britain as a Container: Immigration Metaphors in the 2005 Election Campaign." *Discourse & Society* 17(6): 563–582. doi: 10.1177/0957926506066345

Chilton, Paul. 2004. *Analysing Political Discourse*. London: Routledge.

Clinton, Hillary. 2018. "Transcript. Secretary Hillary Rodham Clinton Remarks at Bonavero Institute of Human Rights." October 9, 2018. Oxford University, Oxford, UK. www.law.ox.ac.uk/sites/files/oxlaw/keynote_speech_by_secretary _hillary_clinton_20181009_0.pdf

Clinton, Hillary, and Tim Kaine. 2016. *Stronger Together: A Blueprint for America's Future*. New York: Simon & Schuster.

Conoscenti, Michelangelo. 2011. *The Reframer: An Analysis of Barack Obama's Political Discourse (2004–2010)*. Roma: Bulzoni.

Coulter, Ann H. 2015. *¡Adios, America!: The Left's Plan to Turn Our Country into a Third World Hellhole*. Washington, DC: Regnery.

Davis, Julie Hirschfeld, and Michael D. Shear. 2019. *Border Wars: Inside Trump's Assault on Immigration*. New York: Simon & Schuster.

De Blij, Harm. 2009. *The Power of Place: Geography, Destiny, and Globalization's Rough Landscape*. New York: Oxford University Press.

De Witte, Melissa. 2021. "President Biden's First Day in Office Signaled a New Era in American Politics, Stanford Scholars Say." *Stanford News*, January 21, 2021. https://news.stanford.edu/2021/01/21/president-bidens-busy-first-day/

Deleixhe, Martin, Magdalena Dembinska and Julien Danero Iglesias. 2019. "Introduction to the Special Issue: Securitized Borderlands." *Journal of Borderland Studies* 34(5): 639–647.

Demata, Massimiliano. 2017. "'A Great and Beautiful Wall': Donald Trump's Populist Discourse on Immigration." *Journal of Language Aggression and Conflict* 5(2): 277–297.

Diener, Alexander C., and Joshua Hagen. 2009. "Theorizing Borders in a 'Borderless World': Globalization, Territory and Identity." *Geography Compass* 3(3): 1196–1216.

Doherty, Carroll. 2016. "5 Facts about Trump Supporters' Views of Immigration." *Pew Research Center*, August 25, 2016. www.pewresearch.org/fact-tank/2016/08/ 25/5-facts-about-trump-supporters-views-of-immigration/

Dovi, Susanne. 2018. "The Ethics of Name-Brand Populism," in "Critical Exchange: Political and Ethical Action in the Age of Trump." *Contemporary Political Theory* 17(3): 331–362.

Dumenco, Simon. 2017. "How to Understand the Trump Brand in 2017." *Advertising Age*, January 9, 2017. http://adage.com/article/media/how-to-understand-the-trump-brand-in-2017/307423/

Emery Jr., Eugene C., and Louis Jacobson. 2016. "Donald Trump's First TV Ad Shows Migrants 'at the Southern Border,' but They're Actually in Morocco." *Politifact*, January 4, 2016. www.politifact.com/factchecks/2016/jan/04/donald-trump/donald-trumps-first-tv-ad-shows-migrants-southern-/

Factbase. 2021. *Donald Trump. Speeches. Tweets. Policy. Unedited. Unfiltered. Instantly*. https://factba.se/trump/

Flowerdew, John. 2004. "The Discursive Construction of a World-Class City." *Discourse and Society* 15(5): 579–605.

Friedman, Nancy. 2015. "Brand Names of the Year for 2015." *Visual Thesaurus*, December 22, 2015. www.visualthesaurus.com/cm/candlepwr/brand-names-of-the-year-for-2015/

Giddens, Anthony. 1984. *The Constitution of Society.* Berkley, CA: University of California Press.

Gramlich, John. 2016. "Trump Voters Want to Build the Wall, but Are More Divided on Other Immigration Questions." *Pew Research Center*, November 29, 2016. www.pewresearch.org/fact-tank/2016/11/29/trump-voters-want-to-build-the-wall-but-are-more-divided-on-other-immigration-questions/

Gramlich, John. 2019. "How Americans See Illegal Immigration, the Border Wall and Political Compromise." *Pew Research Center*, January 16, 2019. www.pewresea rch.org/fact-tank/2019/01/16/how-americans-see-illegal-immigration-the-bor der-wall-and-political-compromise/

Hakim, Denny, and Sui-Lee Wee. 2017. "From Trump the Nationalist, a Trail of Global Trademarks." *New York Times*, February 21, 2017. www.nytimes.com/2017/02/21/business/donald-trump-trademarks-china.html

Hananoki, Eric. 2015. "Ann Coulter Claims Credit for Donald Trump's Anti-Immigrant Bomb Throwing." *Media Matters for America*, July 2, 2015. http://mediamatters.org/blog/2015/07/02/ann-coulter-claims-credit-for-donald-tru mps-ant/204236

Hart, Christopher. 2010. *Critical Discourse Analysis and Cognitive Science: New Perspectives on Immigration Discourse.* Basingstoke: Palgrave. doi: 10.1057/9780230299009

Hassner, Ron E., and Jason Wittenberg. 2015. "Barriers to Entry: Who Builds Fortified Boundaries and Why?" *International Security* 31(3): 157–190. doi: 10.1162/ISEC_a_00206

Hobsbawm, Eric J. 1992. *Nations and Nationalism Since 1780: Programme, Myth, Reality.* Second edition. Cambridge: Cambridge University Press. www.washingtonpost. com/national/trump-wants-his-border-barrier-to-be-painted-black-with-spikes-he-has-other-ideas-too/2019/05/16/b088c07e-7676-11e9-b3f5-5673edf2d12 7_story.html

Hunston, Susan. 2017. "Donald Trump and the Language of Populism." *Perspectives*, University of Birmingham, September 21, 2017. www.birmingham.ac.uk/resea rch/perspective/donald-trump-language-of-populism.aspx

Inglehart, Ronald, and Pippa Norris. 2016. "Trump, Brexit, and the Rise of Populism: Economic Have-Nots and Cultural Backlash." Working paper No. RWP16-026. Harvard Kennedy School. www.hks.harvard.edu/publications/trump-brexit-and-rise-of-populism-economic-have-nots-and-cultural-backlash

Jimenez, Tyler, Jamie Arndt and Mark J. Landau. 2021. "Walls Block Waves: Using an Inundation Metaphor of Immigration Predicts Support for a Border Wall." *Journal of Social and Political Psychology* 9(1): 159–171.

Jones, Reece. 2009. "Geopolitical Boundary Narratives, the Global War on Terror and Border Fencing in India." *Transactions of the Institute of British Geographers* 34(3): 290–304.

Jones, Reece. 2012. *Border Walls. Security and the War on Terror on the United States, India, and Israel.* London and New York: Zed Books.

Jones, Reese, ed. 2019. *Open Borders: In Defense of Free Movement.* Athens, GA: University of Georgia Press.

Keller, Kevin Lane, Susan E. Heckler and Michael J. Houston. 1998. "The Effects of Brand Name Suggestiveness on Advertising Recall." *Journal of Marketing* 62: 48–57.

KhosraviNik, Majid. 2010. "The Representation of Refugees, Asylum Seekers and Immigrants in British Newspapers: A Critical Discourse Analysis." *Journal of Language and Politics* 9(1): 1–28.

Klein, Ezra. 2015. "Bernie Sanders: The Vox Conversation." *Vox*, July 28, 2015. www.vox.com/2015/7/28/9014491/bernie-sanders-vox-conversation

Kohli, Chiranjeev, and Douglas W. LaBahn. 1997. "Creating Effective Brand Names: A Study of the Naming Process." *Journal of Advertising Research* 37(1): 67–75.

Koller, Veronika. 2008. "Corporate Brands as Socio-cognitive Representations." In *Cognitive Sociolinguistics*, ed. by Gitte Kristiansen and René Dirven, 389–418. Berlin: De Gruyter.

Kolossov, Vladimir. 2005. "Border Studies: Changing Perspectives and Theoretical Approaches." *Geopolitics* 10(4): 606–632.

Konrad, Victor. 2014. "Borders, Bordered Lands and Borderlands: Geographical States of Insecurity Between Canada and the United States and the Impacts of Security Primacy." In *Borders, Fences and Walls. States of Insecurity?*, ed. by Elisabeth Vallet, 85–102. London and New York: Routledge.

Krzyżanowski, Michal. 2016. "Recontextualisation of Neoliberalism and the Increasingly Conceptual Nature of Discourse: Challenges for Critical Discourse Studies." *Discourse & Society* 27(3): 308–321.

Lakoff, George. 2002. *Moral Politics: How Liberals and Conservatives Think*. Second edition. Chicago and London: University of Chicago Press.

Lemon, Jason. 2019. "Bernie Sanders Says U.S. Can't Have 'Open Borders' Because Poor People Will Come 'From All Over the World.'" *Newsweek*, April 8, 2019. www.newsweek.com/brnie-sanders-open-borders-poverty-world-immigration-1388767

Levy, Sidney. 1978. *Marketplace Behavior: Its Meaning for Management*. New York: AMACOM.

Lischinsky, Alon. 2018. "Critical Discourse Analysis and Branding." In *The Routledge Handbook of Critical Discourse Studies*, ed. by John Flowerdew and John E. Richardson, 540–553. London: Routledge.

Lorenzo-Dus, Nuria. 2006. "Buying and Selling: Mediating Persuasion in British Property Shows." *Media Culture & Society* 28(5): 739–761.

Luntz, Frank. 2007. *Words that Work: It's Not What You Say, It's What People Hear*. New York: Hyperion.

Marx, Anthony W. 2002. "The Nation-State and Its Exclusions." *Political Science Quarterly* 117(1): 103–126.

May, Elaine Tyler. 2003. "'Family Values': The Uses and Abuses of American Family History." *Revue Francaise d'Etudes Americaines* 97: 7–22.

Mayer, Jane. 2016. "Donald Trump's Ghostwriter Tells All." *The New Yorker*, July 25, 2016. www.newyorker.com/magazine/2016/07/25/donald-trumps-ghostwriter-tells-all

Mazzarella, William. 2019. "Brand(ish)ing the Name. Or, Why Is Trump so Enjoyable?" In *Sovereignty, Inc.: Three Inquiries in Politics and Enjoyment*, ed. by William Mazzarella, Eric L. Santer and Aaron Schuster, 113–160. Chicago: University of Chicago Press.

Miroff, Nick, and Josh Dawsey. 2019. "Trump Wants His Border Barrier To Be Painted Black with Spikes: He Has Other Ideas, Too." *Washington Post*, May 16, 2019.

Mitsikopoulou, Bessie. 2008. "Introduction: The Branding of Political Entities as Discursive Practice." *Journal of Language and Politics* 7(3): 353–371.

Moffitt, Benjamin. 2016, *The Global Rise of Populism. Performance, Political Style, and Representation.* Stanford: Stanford University Press.

Monmouth University Poll. 2015. "Split Decision on Mexico Border Wall." *Monmouth University Polling Institute*, September 10, 2015. www.monmouth.edu/polling-institute/reports/MonmouthPoll_US_091015/

Nagle, Angela. 2018. "The Left Case Against Open Borders." *American Affairs* 2(4): 17–30. https://americanaffairsjournal.org/2018/11/the-left-case-against-open-borders/#notes.

Newman, David. 2006. "The Lines that Continue to Separate Us: Borders in our 'Borderless' World." *Progress in Human Geography* 30(2): 143–161.

Newman, David, and Anssi Paasi. 1998. "Fences and Neighbours in the Postmodern World: Boundary Narratives in Political Geography." *Progress in Human Geography* 22(2): 186–207.

Ohmae, Kenichi. 1995. *The End of the Nation-State.* New York: Free Press.

O'Shaughnessy, Nicholas. 2001. "The Marketing of Political Marketing." *European Journal of Marketing* 35(9–10): 1047–1057.

Peters, Jeremy. 2017. "Conservatives Recoil at Trump's Accommodation with Democrats over DACA." *New York Times*, September 14, 2017. www.nytimes.com/2017/09/14/us/politics/conservatives-trump-democrats-daca.html

Pryce, Gwilym, and Sarah Oates. 2008. "Rhetoric in the Language of Real Estate Marketing." *Housing Studies* 23(2): 319–348.

Qiu, Linda. 2018. "No, Democrats Don't Want 'Open Borders.'" *New York Times*, June 7, 2018. www.nytimes.com/2018/06/27/us/politics/fast-check-donald-trump-democrats-open-borders.html

Rasmussen Reports. 2015. "Voters Want to Build a Wall, Deport Felon Illegal Immigrants." *Rasmussen Reports*, August 19, 2015. www.rasmussenreports.com/public_content/politics/current_events/immigration/august_2015/voters_want_to_build_a_wall_deport_felon_illegal_immigrants.

Ratner, Abraham. 2020. "Trumpism Is an Aesthetic, Not an Ideology—and It Will Survive Donald Trump." *Salon*, July 19, 2020. www.salon.com/2020/07/19/trumpism-is-an-aesthetic-not-an-ideology--and-it-will-survive-donald-trump/

Reisigl, Martin. 2008. "Analyzing Political Rhetoric." In *Qualitative Discourse Analysis in the Social Sciences*, ed. by Ruth Wodak and Michal Krzyżanowski, 96–120. London: Palgrave.

Reisigl, Martin, and Ruth Wodak. 2001. *Discourse and Discrimination. Rhetorics of Racism and Antisemitism.* London and New York: Routledge.

Reisigl, Martin, and Ruth Wodak. 2016. "The Discourse-Historical Approach (DHA)." In *Methods of Critical Discourse Studies*, third edition, ed. by Ruth Wodak and Michael Meyer, 23–61. London: Sage.

Sanders, Bernie. 2020. "A Welcoming and Safe America for All." Bernie Sanders Official Website. https://berniesanders.com/issues/welcoming-and-safe-america-all/

Santa Ana, Otto. 1999. "'Like an Animal I Was Treated': Anti-immigrant Metaphor in US Public Discourse." *Discourse & Society* 10: 191–224.

Scammell, Margaret. 2007. "Political Brands and Consumer Citizens: The Rebranding of Tony Blair." *Annals of the American Academy of Political and Social Science* 611: 176–192.

Schuster, Aaron. 2017. "Primal Scream; or, Why Do Babies Cry? A Theory of Trump." *e-flux* 83. www.e-flux.com/journal/83/140999/primal-scream-or-why-do-babies-cry-a-theory-of-trump/

Semino, Elena. 2008. *Metaphor in Discourse*. Cambridge: Cambridge University Press.

Sherman, Amy. 2016. "Donald Trump Says Hillary Clinton Would Create 'Totally Open Borders.'" *Politifact*, June 23, 2016. www.politifact.com/factchecks/2016/jun/23/donald-trump/donald-trump-says-hillary-clinton-would-create-tot/

Sides, John. 2018. "The Extraordinary Unpopularity of Trump's Family Separation Policy (in One Graph)." *Washington Post*, June 19, 2018. www.washingtonpost.com/news/monkey-cage/wp/2018/06/19/the-extraordinary-unpopularity-of-trumps-family-separation-policy-in-one-graph/

Stacey, Judith. 1996. *In the Name of the Family: Rethinking Family Values in the Postmodern Age*. Boston: Beacon.

Steele, Brent J., and Alexandra Homolar. 2019. "Ontological Insecurities and the Politics of Contemporary Populism." Special issue of *Cambridge Review of International Affairs* 32(3): 214–221.

Talbot, Margaret. 2018. "The Trump's Administration's Family Values." *The New Yorker*, June 24, 2018. www.newyorker.com/magazine/2018/07/02/the-trump-administrations-family-values

Todd, Sarah. 2017. "21 Unexpected Things that Donald Trump Thinks Are Beautiful." *Quartz*, September 26, 2017. https://qz.com/1086942/21-unexpected-things-that-donald-trump-thinks-are-beautiful/

Trump, Donald J. 2015a. *Crippled America. How to Make America Great Again*. New York: Threshold.

Trump, Donald J. 2015b. "Immigration Reform That Will Make America Great Again." August 2015. www.donaldjtrump.com/positions/immigration-reform

Trump, Donald J. 2015c. *The Late Show with Stephen Colbert*, "Donald Trump Has Nothing to Apologize for." September 22, 2015. www.youtube.com/watch?v=Ns7ocpRhDD8

Trump, Donald J. 2015d. *Donald J. Trump Facebook Page*. November 22, 2015. www.facebook.com/DonaldTrump/photos/a.488852220724.393301.153080620724/10156337706805725/

Trump, Donald J. 2016a. "2016 Political Ad by Donald J. Trump for President." January 27, 2016. https://archive.org/details/PolAd_DonaldTrump_5iqfp

Trump, Donald J. 2016b. "Statement on New Census Data Showing Record Immigration Growth." March 7, 2016. www.donaldjtrump.com/press-releases/donald-j.-trumpstatement-on-immigration

Trump, Donald J., Wynton Hall, Peter Schweizer and Meredith McIver. 2011. *Time to Get Tough: Making America #1 Again*. Washington, DC: Regnery.

Trump, Donald J., and Meredith McIver. 2004. *Trump: How to Get Rich*. New York: Random House.

Trump, Donald J., and Tony Schwartz. 1987. *Trump: The Art of the Deal*. New York: Ballantine Books-Random House.

Trump White House Archived. 2022. https://trumpwhitehouse.archives.gov/

Vaillancourt, William. 2017. "The Great Destroyer: Donald Trump's Contempt for Aesthetics." *The Progressive*, August 1, 2017. https://progressive.org/magazine/the-great-destroyer-donald-trump%E2%80%99s-contempt-for-aesthetics/

Vallet, Elisabeth, ed. 2014. *Borders, Fences and Walls. States of insecurity?* London and New York: Routledge.

Van Dijk, Teun A. 1991. "The Interdisciplinary Study of News as Discourse." In *Handbook of Qualitative Methods in Mass Communication Research*, ed. by Klaus Bruhn-Jensen and Nicholas W. Jankowski, 108–120. London: Routledge.

Van Dijk, Teun A. 2000. "New(s) Racism: A Discourse Analytical Approach." In *Ethnic Minorities and the Media*, ed. by Simon Cottle, 33–49. Milton Keynes: Open University Press.

Van Dijk, Teun A. 2005. "Politics, Ideology and Discourse." In *Elsevier Encyclopedia of Language and Linguistics. Politics and Language*, ed. by Ruth Wodak, 728–740. Oxford: Elsevier.

Van Gelder, Sicco. 2002. "A View on the Future of Branding." *Brand Meta: Global Brand Strategy*. https://incitrio.com/docs/View_on_Future_of_Branding.pdf

Van Ham, Peter. 2001. "The Rise of the Brand State." *Foreign Affairs*, September/October 2001. www.foreignaffairs.org

Van Ham, Peter. 2002. "Branding Territory: Inside the Wonderful Worlds of PR and IR Theory." *Millennium Journal of International Studies* 31 (2): 249–269.

Van Houtum, Henk. 2005. "The Geopolitics of Borders and Boundaries." *Geopolitics* 10(4): 672–679.

Van Houtum, Henk, and Tom van Naerssen. 2001. "Bordering Ordering and Othering." *Tijdschrift voor Economische en Sociale Geografie* 93(2): 125–136.

Wagner, Alex. 2018. "The Republican Party Moves from Family Values to White Nationalism." *The Atlantic*, June 22, 2018. www.theatlantic.com/ideas/archive/2018/06/the-gop-has-chosen-white-nationalism-over-family-values/563429/

White, Jon, and Leslie De Chernatony. 2002. "New Labour: A Study of the Creation, Development and Demise of a Political Brand." *Journal of Political Marketing* 1(2–3): 45–52.

White House. 2021a. "Proclamation on the Termination of Emergency with Respect to the Southern Border of the United States and Redirection of Funds Diverted to Border Wall Construction." The White House, January 20, 2021. www.whitehouse.gov/briefing-room/presidential-actions/2021/01/20/proclamation-termination-of-emergency-with-respect-to-southern-border-of-united-states-and-redirection-of-funds-diverted-to-border-wall-construction/

White House. 2021b. "Fact Sheet: President Biden Sends Immigration Bill to Congress as Part of His Commitment to Modernize Our Immigration System." The White House, January 20, 2021. www.whitehouse.gov/briefing-room/ statements-releases/2021/01/20/fact-sheet-president-biden-sends-immigrat ion-bill-to-congress-as-part-of-his-commitment-to-modernize-our-immigration-system/

White House. 2021c. "FACT SHEET: The Biden Administration Blueprint for a Fair, Orderly and Humane Immigration System." The White House, July 27, 2021. www.whitehouse.gov/briefing-room/statements-releases/2021/07/27/ fact-sheet-the-biden-administration-blueprint-for-a-fair-orderly-and-humane-immigration-system/

White House. 2021d. "FACT SHEET: The Collaborative Migration Management Strategy." The White House, July 27, 2021. www.whitehouse.gov/briefing-room/statements-releases/2021/07/29/fact-sheet-the-collaborative-migration-management-strategy/

Wikileaks. 2016. "HRC Paid Speeches." *Wikileaks*, January 25, 2016. https://wikile aks.org/podesta-emails/emailid/927

Wikipedia. 2020. "Trump Wall." https://en.wikipedia.org/wiki/Trump_wall

Winston, David. 2017. "Placing Priority: How Issues Mattered More than Demographics in the 2016 Election." *Voter Study Group*, December 2017. www. voterstudygroup.org/publication/placing-priority

Wodak, Ruth. 2001. "The Discourse-Historical Approach." In *Methods of Critical Discourse Analysis*, ed. by Ruth Wodak, and Michael Meyer, 63–94. London: Sage.

Wodak, Ruth. 2010. "The Discursive Construction of History. Brief Considerations." *Mots* 94: 57–65.

Wodak, Ruth. 2015. *The Politics of Fear*. London: Sage.

Wodak Ruth, and Norman Fairclough. 2010. "Recontextualizing European Higher Education Policies: the Cases of Austria and Romania." *Critical Discourse Studies* 7(1): 19–40. doi: 10.1080/17405900903453922

Wodak, Ruth, Rudolf de Cillia, Martin Reisigl and Karin Liebhart. 2009. *The Discursive Construction of National Identity*. Second edition. Edinburgh: University Press.

Index